COUNTY SOU]
SOCIETY OF G]

NORFOLK

Series editor
Neville Taylor FSG

Parish registers
Nonconformist registers
Marriage licences

Society of Genealogists 2000

Published by
Society of Genealogists Enterprises Limited
14 Charterhouse Buildings
Goswell Road
London EC1M 7BA

© Society of Genealogists 2000

ISBN 1 903462 25 8

British Library Cataloguing in Publication Data
A CIP Catalogue record for this book is available from the British Library

Society of Genealogists Enterprises Limited is a wholly owned subsidiary of
Society of Genealogists, a registered charity, no 233701

INTRODUCTION

This booklet is one of a series of guides to parts of the Society of Genealogists collections. The layout is similar to that of the book in the Library Sources series entitled *Parish Register Copies in the Library of the Society of Genealogists.*

CONTENT
Details are kept to the minimum necessary to indicate whether the Society possesses material for a particular place and, if so, the time period covered. Note that no distinction is made as to the nature of the material listed which may be transcriptions of Parish Registers or Bishop's Transcripts or, in the case of microforms, reproductions of the original documents. Marriages included in *Boyd's Marriage Index* are indicated by [Boyd] after the dates.

USING THIS GUIDE TO FIND MATERIAL IN THE LIBRARY
For bound material, most entries show the library shelf numbers. Where no such number is indicated, the material may be available only on application to staff or it may have been temporarily withdrawn for typing, indexing or binding. In addition a number of transcripts are to be found in periodicals which have not been given a unique shelf number. In all cases where a unique shelf number is not shown, please refer to the library's computerised catalogue to help find the item. For material in the form of microfilm (Mf), the film number is given and microfilms are accessible in the film reading room. For microfiche (Mfc), the number shown may be used to apply to library staff for the item.

PARISH NAMES
In the case of those which include an additional physical description eg. Upper, Great, North, Old, etc., the name is usually given first followed by the description (eg Dalby, Great) so that all occurrences of the name in a county appear together. The dedications of parish churches are included where they are identified in the original material. Indexes are included even if there is no complete transcript but banns are included only where they extend the coverage relating to marriages.

LOANS
Members of the Society resident in the United Kingdom are permitted to borrow certain items from the Library. No indication is given in this booklet as to the availability of any item for loan and loans are made at the discretion of the Librarian to whom enquiries should be made.

ACKNOWLEDGMENTS
The Society of Genealogists thanks Violet Shaw for assistance given in processing text exported from the computer catalogue to produce this guide.

Neville C Taylor FSG
Series Editor

ABBREVIATIONS

a. general abbreviations

Z	Births	**C**	Baptisms
A	Adult Baptisms	**M**	Marriages
D	Deaths	**B**	Burials
(I)	Index only	**Ext**	Extracts only
ST	Saint (in a place name)	**St**	Saint (church dedication)

b. non-conformists

Bapt	Baptist	**Bible Christ**	Bible Christian
Calv	Calvinistic	**Cong**	Congregationalist
Diss	Dissenting	**Episc**	Episcopalian
Franc	Franciscan	**Hug**	Huguenot
Ind	Independent		
Lady Hunt Conn	Lady Huntingdon's Connexion		
Luth	Lutheran	**Meth**	Methodist
New Conn	New Connexion	**Part Bapt**	Particular Baptist
Plym Breth	Plymouth Brethren	**Presb**	Presbyterian
Prim Meth	Primitive Methodist	**Prot**	Protestant
Rom Cath	Roman Catholic	**SFrs**	Society of Friends (Quaker)
Unit	Unitarian	**Wes**	Wesleyan

c. locating material in the library

[xx] Numbers in square brackets are the shelf numbers of bound material in the Society's collections within the **[R]**egisters section of the county. The addition of a two letter prefix indicates that the material is to be found in the collection of a different county. Some register copies are NOT in the **[R]**egisters section and this case their location is shown by a letter preceding the number: **[G]**eneral, **[L]**ocal, **[M]**onumental Inscriptions or in the case of periodicals **[PER]**.

Mf xxxx Microfilm with film number - available for self selection in the microfilm reading room.

Mfc xxxxx Microfiche with fiche reference - available on completion of a request slip and application to staff at the Library Counter

AS	Apply to staff	**CRS**	Catholic Record Society
HS	Huguenot Society	**HarS**	Harleian Society
GCI	Great Card Index at the Society of Genealogists, entries are on slips which are sorted by surname and forename.		

Note

The listings include accessions up to 12 July 2000

National index of parish registers, vol. 7 East Anglia: Cambridgeshire, Norfolk & Suffolk [Textbook shelves]

International Genealogical Index of Births Baptisms & Marriages (Mfc) [IGI Cabinet]
International Genealogical Index & addendum (CD-ROM) [AS]

Norfolk genealogy vol. 14 amendments & additions to Norwich marriage index 1813-37 [Shelf 9]
Index to Bishops Transcripts from the Diocese of Norwich 1685-91, 1705, 1715 [80]
An index of stray registrations, vol. 1 CMB(I) Ext 1558-1834 (Norfolk entries) [UK/REG]
East Anglian marriages mainly before 1700 series 1 [SF/R 285]
East Anglian marriages before 1812 series 2 [SF/R 286]
East Anglian stray marriages 1538-1860 [Mfc 91261]
Marriage & obituary notices 1848, 1851, 1880, 1881, 1882, 1890, 1900 (Lynn Advertiser - Norfolk) [70]
Parish registers & transcripts in the Norfolk Record Office 1994 [AS]
Quaker digest registers of births, marriages & burials - Norfolk & Norwich Quarterly Meeting: Z 1613-1837 & 1689-1795, M 1658-1836 & 1693-1801, B 1657-1837 & 1688-1806 [Mf 3368]

ACLE C(I) 1664-1847 [Mf 1423]; M 1664-1815 [AS]; M(I) 1664-1812 [Boyd]

ACRE, SOUTH M(I) 1576-1812 [Boyd]

ACRE, WEST CMB 1665-1812 [Mf 1087]; M(I) 1668-1837 [Boyd]

ALBURGH M(I) 1541-1753 [Boyd]

ALBY C 1558-1983 M 1558-1725 1754-1837 B 1558-1981 [Mf 1640]

ALBY with THWAITE CMB 1675-1812 [91]

ALDBOROUGH CMB 1725-1812 [90] M(I) 1538-1715 [Boyd]; M(I) 1747-1811 [PER]

ALDEBY BY HADDISCOE C Ext 1566-1649 M Ext 1558-1793 B Ext 1566-1811 [Mf 1043]

ALDERFORD C 1723-1812 M 1727-1812 1824-36 B 1726-1812 [Mfc 66591]

ANMER M 1600-1837 [67] M(I) 1709 1835 [Boyd]

ANTINGHAM C 1679-1704/05 1740-1812 B 1680-1812 M 1680-1753 [Mf 987]; C Ext 1679-1801 M Ext 1680-1753 B Ext 1680/81-1812 [Mf 1043]; CMB 1726-1812 [89]; M(I) 1680-1754 [Boyd]

ARMINGHALL C 1558-1735 M 1560-1759 B 1560-1698 [Mf 1641]; M 1570-1641 1657-1676 1690-1754 [Mf 1092] M(I) 1570-1754 [Boyd]

ASHBY (by Loddon) **St Mary** C Ext 1620-1743 M Ext 1623-1744 B Ext 1624-1742 [Mf 1043]; C 1620-1874 M 1621-1839 B 1623-1812 banns 1766-1935 [Mf 1532]

ASHMANHAUGH M(I) 1563-1837 [Boyd]

ASHWICKEN with LEZIATE M 1717-1815 [65]

ASHWICKEN M(I) 1716-1837 [Boyd]

ASMANHAUGH C 1562-1812 M 1562-1836 B 1562-1811 1763 [Mf 987]

ATTLEBOROUGH CMB 1552-1840 [PER]

ATTLEBRIDGE C 1712-1812 M 1725-1835 B 1716-1812 [Mfc 66593]; C 1712-1842 M 1725-1837 B 1716-1842 [96]

AYLMERTON C 1696-1813 1832-1905 M 1696-1924 B 1696-1897 [Mfc 66594]; CMB 1725-1812 [87]; CMB 1731-32 [89]

BABINGLEY M 1694-1805[AS]; M(I) 1662-1812 [Boyd]

BACONSTHORPE C 1682-1726 MB 1682-1725 [Mf 1646]; CMB 1710-11 1747-1812 [86]

BACTON B 1826-36 Bapt [Mfc 91247]; CB 1558-1812 M 1559-1812 [Mf 987]; CMB Ext 1558-1812 [Mf 1043]; M(I) 1559-1812 [Boyd]

BAGTHORPE M 1562-1644 1656-1837 [67]; M(I) 1562-1837 [Boyd]

BALE (alias BATCHLEY) & GUNTHORPE Index to names & periods in which they occur in the parish registers [83]

BARNEY C 1538-1712 M 1542-1709/10 B 1538-1786 [Mf 1095]

BARNINGHAM, LITTLE CMB 1717-1812 [92]

BARNINGHAM, NORTH see BARNINGHAM NORWOOD

BARNINGHAM NORWOOD CB 1538-1695 1714-1812 M 1538-1693 1724-53 B 1538-1695 1710-1812 [Mf 1095]; CMB 1726-1810 [90]; C 1538-1665 1676-89 1714-1908 M 1539-1644 1666-88 1723-54 1848-75 1892-1903 B 1538-1648 1661-85 1710-1956 [Mfc 66595]; C 1813-99 M 1814-92 B 1813-1900 [86]

BARNINGHAM WINTER CMB 1725-1812 [90]

BARSHAM, EAST & NORTH CB 1849 1813-71 [Mfc 73216]

BARSHAM, EAST C 1725-1811 M 1726-68 1787-1811 B 1725-1812 [97]; M 1658-1837 [61]; M(I) 1658-1837 [Boyd]

BARSHAM, NORTH C 1726-1812 M 1726-1810 B 1726-1812 [97]; M 1557-1607 1619-1837 [61]; M(I) 1557-1837 [Boyd]

BARSHAM, WEST C 1756-1811 M 1774-1810 B 1774-1809 [97]; C 1756-1851 M 1813-51 B 1764-1851 [83]; CB 1849 & 1852 1813-71 [Mfc 73216]; M 1813-37 [61]; M(I) 1813-37 [Boyd]

BARTON BENDISH CMB 1695-1733 [Mf 1647]

BARTON BENDISH All Saints with St Mary CMB 1691-1837 [49]

BARTON BENDISH St Andrew C

1706-68 M 1562-64 1695-1718 B 1705-68 [Mf 1093]; CMB 1691-1837 [49]

BARTON TURF M 1558-1837 [59]; M(I) 1558-1836 [Boyd]

BATCHLEY see BALE

BAWBURGH C 1555-1802 M 1565-1812 B 1557-1809 [Mf 1642]; CB 1849 1813-71 [Mfc 73216]

BAWSEY C 1539-1771 B 1539-1771 [Mf 1087]; CM 1539-1771 B 1539-1773 [72]; M 1539-63 1585-1726 1759-71 [65]; M 1539-1651 1660-1729 1739-71 [AS]; M(I) 1539-1771 [Boyd]

BEACHAMWELL see BEECHAMWELL

BECKHAM, WEST CMB 1724-25 1770-75 1779-1812 [87]; M 1689-1836 [AS]; M(I) 1689-1836 [Boyd]

BEDINGHAM CB 1849 1813-71 [Mfc 73216]; M 1561-1812 [59]; M(I) 1561-1812 [Boyd]

BEECHAMWELL C 1558-1901 M 1558-1836 B 1558-1812 [8]; M 1558-1642 1738-1836 [Mf 1095]; M 1558-1642 1738-1836 [47]; CMB Ext 1570-1791 [Mf 1043]

BEESTON BY MILEHAM St Mary CMB Ext 1538-1693 [20]; M 1538-1685 1695-1753 [Mf 1095]; M(I) 1538-1753 [Boyd]

BEESTON REGIS All Saints C 1744-1853 M 1743-1851 B 1743-1852 [107]; CB 1743-1810 M 1743-1812 [At binding]; CB(I) 1743-1810 M(I) 1754-1812 [25]; CMB 1723 1738/39 [Mf 987]

BEESTON St Lawrence C 1558-70 1581-1646 1661-1713/14 1743-1812 M 1558-1652 1660-1712 1734 1739-84 1799-1801 1813-38 B 1558-1646 1658-1712 1743-96 1806-09 [Mf 988]; C 1558-1713 M 1558-1712 B 1559-1712 [Mf 1628]; M(I) 1558-1838 [Boyd]

BEETLEY CMB Ext 1539-1779 [20]

BEIGHTON BY SELE C Ext 1602-1870 M Ext 1612-35 1659-1834 B Ext 1591 1610-1880 [Mf 1095]; M(I) 1589-1745 [Boyd]

BERGH APTON CB 1849 1813-71 [Mfc 73216]; M 1556-1753 [Mf 1092]; M(I)

1556-1753 [Boyd]

BESSINGHAM C 1695-1707 1733-1837 M 1695-1707 1733-1832 banns 1754-1843 B 1695-1707 1734-1838 [Mf 1643]; CMB 1725-1812 [87]

BESTHORPE C 1559-1725 M 1559-1640 1677-1725 B 1558-1649 1677-1725 [Mf 1644]; CB 1841 1849 1857 1813-71 [Mfc 73216]

BEXWELL CB 1857 1813-71 [Mfc 73216]; CMB 1558-1837 [85]

BILLINGFORD St Peter CMB 1739-4 [Mf 987]

BILLINGFORD NEAR DISS St Leonard M(I) 1640-1753 [Boyd]

BILLINGFORD with LITTLE THORPE CB 1841 1849 1857 1866-71 [Mfc 73216]

BILLOCKBY C 1563-1805 M 1561-1748 B 1561-1811 [Mf 1092]; M 1561-1748 [62]; M(I) 1561-1748 [Boyd]

BINHAM C 1559-1653 1702-49 1782-1876 M 1560-1643 1702-48 1754-1837 banns 1755-1909 B 1559-1644 1702-49 1782-1903 [Mfc 66596]

BINTREE C 1582-1899 M 1593-1667 1681-1706 1713-1836 banns 1686-1903 B 1558-1903 [Mfc 70678]

BINTRY *see* BINTREE

BIRCHAM, GREAT CB 1841 1857 1871 [Mfc 73216]; M(I) 1669-1837 [Boyd]

BIRCHAM, GREAT St Mary M 1669-1837 [67]

BIRCHAM NEWTON C 1562-1727 M 1562-1640 1673-1718 1739-43 B 1562-1640 1652-53 1669-1717 1734-38 [48]; CB 1839 1841 1849 1857 1864-71 [Mfc 73216]; M 1562-1640 1673-1836 [67]; M(I) 1562-1837 [Boyd]

BIRCHAM TOFTS CB 1839 1841 1857 1871 [Mfc 73216]; M 1698-1837 [67]; M(I) 1715-1837 [Boyd]

BIXLEY C 1575-1809 M 1563-1732 B Ext 1578-1762 [Mf 1046]; C Ext 1576-1809 M Ext 1563-1706 B Ext 1593-1796 [Mf 1095]; CMB 1820 CB 1857 1871 [Mfc 73216]; M(I) 1561-1738 [Boyd]

BLAKENEY CMB 1696-1789 [87]

BLICKLING C Ext 1559-1811 M Ext 1567-1823 B Ext 1560-1812 [Mf 1095]

BLO NORTON CB 1562-1725 M 1562-1725 1758-1812 banns 1758-1847 [Mf 1645]; CMB 1820 CB 1839-41 1849 1857 1871 1813-71 [Mfc 73216]

BLO NORTON St Andrew C 1813-87 M 1813-36 [Mf 3395]

BLOFIELD C 1545-1901 M 1547-1915 B 1546-1901 [Mfc 66619]; C(I) 1548-1812 [Mf 988]; M(I) 1547-1786 [Boyd]

BODHAM CMB 1729-1812 [89]

BODNEY CMB 1653-1837 [49]; CMB 1735-40 [Mf 987]; CMB 1820 CB 1857 1871 [Mfc 73216]

BOOTON M 1560-1666 1676-81 1723-1812 [AS]; M(I) 1560-1812 [Boyd]

BOUGHTON CMB 1691-1837 [49]

BOUGHTON All Saints CMB 1814 1820 1836 CB 1839-41 1849 1851-52 1855-57 1813-71 [Mfc 73216]

BRACON ASH CMB 1814 1820 1832 1836 CB 1839-41 1849 1851-52 1868-71 [Mfc 73216]

BRADENHAM, EAST CMB 1814 1820 1828 1831-32 1836 CB 1839-41 1843 1849 1851-52 1855-57 [Mfc 73216]; Z 1691-1714 CM 1714-1812 B 1695-1812 [Mf 1648]

BRADENHAM, WEST C 1538-1901 M 1539-1902 B 1643-90 1813-1902 [Mfc 66620]; CB 1538-1812 M 1538-1646 1676-1789 [Mf 1649]; CMB 1814 1820 1823 1826 1828 1830-32 CB 1843 1851 1855 [Mfc 73216]

BRADESTONE M(I) 1623-1812 [Boyd]

BRADFIELD C 1726-1812 MB 1725-1812 [Mf 988]; CMB 1725-1812 [89]; CMB 1814-15 1818 1820 1823 1826 1828-32 1834-36 CB 1839-41 1843-44 1849 1851-52 [Mfc 73216]; M(I) 1725-1812 [Boyd]

BRADISTON *see* BRADESTONE

BRAMERTON C 1551-1751 M 1551-1739 B 1551-1733 [Mf 1650]; CMB 1814-15 1818 1820 1823 1825-26 1828-32 1834-36 CB 1855-57 1866-71 [Mfc 73216]; M(I) 1566-1749 [Boyd]

BRAMPTON C 1732-1812 M 1732-1810 B 1732-1811 [6]; M(I) 1654-1812

[Boyd]

BRANCASTER CMB 1814-15 1818 1820 1822-23 1825-26 1828-36 CB 1837 1840 1842-44 1851-52 1855-57 [Mfc 73216]

BRANDISTON CB 1562-1902 M 1565-1901 banns 1823-1904 [Mfc 66621]

BRANDON PARVA CMB 1813-15 1817-18 1820 1822-23 1825-26 1828-36 CB 1837-40 1842-44 1849 1852 1856 1871 [Mfc 73216]

BRAYDESTON M 1623-1812 [AS]

BRESSINGHAM CMB 1813-15 1817-35 CB 1839-40 1842-44 1851-52 1855-57 [Mfc 73216] M(I) 1559-1753 [Boyd]

BRETTENHAM CMB 1725-1812 [Mfc 73217]; CMB 1813-14 1817-36 CB 1837-44 1848-49 1851-52 1855-57 1865-71 [Mfc 73216]

BRIDGHAM C 1558-1737 M 1558-1736 B 1558-1728 [Mf 1619]; C 1588-1899 M 1558-1686 1691-1788 1813-1930 B 1558-1812) [Mfc 78232]; CMB 1815 1818 1828-29 1836 CB 1839 [Mfc 73216]

BRININGHAM CMB 1719-1812 [95]

BRINTON CB 1706-1812 M 1730-1810 [91]

BROCKDISH CMB 1813-15 1817-27 1829-36 CB 1837-43 [Mfc 73216]; M(I) 1559-1754 [Boyd]

BROOKE CMB 1813 1815 1817-19 1821-27 1829-1831 1833-36 CB 1837-38 1840-44 1856 [Mfc 73216]; M(I) 1558-1812 [Boyd]

BROOME CMB 1813 1817-19 1821-27 1829-30 1833-35 CB 1837-38 1840-44 1848 1851-52 1855-57 [Mfc 73216]; M 1761-1812 [91]; M(I) 1538-1760 [Boyd]

BRUMSTEAD St Peter C 1562-1618 1625-39 1645-1812 M 1561-98 1627-35 1651-61 1672-79 1695-1732 1740-1845 B 1561-96 1625-39 1653-61 1666-1812 [113]; C 1561-1812 M 1561-98 1627-35 1651-61 1672-79 1695-1845 B 1561-96 1625-39 1653-1812 1716 1791 [Mf 991]; C(I) 1562-1812 [Mf 1419]; C 1562-1812 M 1561-1949 B 1561-1812 [Mfc 66622]; CMB 1813 1817-19 1821-27 1829-30 1833-35 CB 1837-38 1840-44 1848-49 1851-52 1855-57 1871 [Mfc 73216]; M(I) 1562-1837 [Boyd]

BRUNDALL M 1563-1812 [AS]; M(I) 1566-1812 [Boyd]

BUCKENHAM, NEW CMB 1813 1817-19 1821-27 1829-30 1833-35 CB 1837-38 1842-44 1848-49 1851-52 1855-57 1871 [Mfc 73216]

BUCKENHAM, OLD CMB 1537-1691 [Mf 1651]; CMB 1560-1649 [68]; CMB 1813 1817 1819 1821-25 1827 CB 1837-38 1842 1844 1848 1851-52 1855-57 [Mfc 73216]; M(I) 1560-1649 [Boyd]

BUCKENHAM TOFTS see TOFTS, WEST

BUNWELL CMB 1813 1817 1819 1821 1824-25 1827 CB 1837-38 1844 1848 1851 1856-57 [Mfc 73216]

BURGH ST MARGARET C 1787-1829 M 1822-37 B 1790-1863 [Mf 1094]; CMB 1746-47 1769-70 [Mf 987]; M 1813-37 [62]; M(I) 1813-37 [Boyd]

BURGH ST PETER CMB 1821 1824 1827 CB 1838 1844 1848 1851 1857 [Mfc 73216]; M(I) 1560-1812 [Boyd]

BURLINGHAM, NORTH see **BURLINGHAM ST ANDREW or BURLINGHAM ST PETER**

BURLINGHAM ST ANDREW CB 1538-1884 M 1538-1837 banns 1756-1812 [Mf 1094]; C 1539-1812 M 1543-1812 B 1546-1812 [Mf 1046]; M 1540-1812 [AS]; M(I) 1540-1812 [Boyd]

BURLINGHAM ST PETER CMB Ext 1539-60 C 1560-1884 M 1560-1730 1746 1754-1812 banns 1754-1834 B 1561-1884 [Mf 1094]; C 1560-1784 M 1586-1807 B 1585-1780 [Mf 1046]; M 1500-1812 [AS]; M(I) 1560-1812 [Boyd]

BURNHAM DEEPDALE CMB 1821 1824 CB 1838 1848 1857 [Mfc 73216]; M 1538-1652 1662-1753 [Mf 1094]; M(I) 1539-1753 [Boyd]

BURNHAM NORTON CMB 1821 CB 1838 1848 [Mfc 73216]

BURNHAM OVERY CB 1838 1848 [Mfc 73216]

BURNHAM SUTTON M(I) 1653-1837 [Boyd]

BURNHAM SUTTON with ULPH M

1653-1837 [59]; CMB 1725/26-1812 [95]; CB 1848 [Mfc 73216]

BURNHAM THORPE CMB 1819 CB 1848 1857 [Mfc 73216]

BURNHAM WESTGATE CB 1848 1857 [Mfc 73216]

BURSTON C 1654-1812 M 1654-1814 B 1655-1812 [Mf 3481]; C 1668-89 B 1662 (Ext for Claxton only) [113]; CB 1857 [Mfc 73216]; M(I) 1645-1753 [Boyd]

BUXTON CMB 1600-09 1623-24 1628-29 1633-34 1665-1758 CB 1758-1812; [100]

CAISTER St Edmund CMB 1557-1719 [Mf 1047]; CB 1857 [Mfc 73216]; M(I) 1557-1810 [Boyd]

CAISTOR NEXT YARMOUTH see CAISTOR ON SEA

CAISTOR ON SEA C 1558-1737 B 1550-1812 [Mf 1046]; C Ext 1593-1812 M Ext 1572-1831 B Ext 1565-1812 [Mf 1046]; M 1563-1837 [62]; M(I) 1563-1837 [Boyd]

CALTHORPE C 1696-1812 M 1703-1811 B 1696-1811 [91]; M 1558-1812 [AS]; M(I) 1558-1812 [Boyd]

CANTLEY CB 1813-37 M 1813-35 [83]

CARLETON, EAST CB 1857 [Mfc 73216]

CARLETON FOREHOE CB 1857 [Mfc 73216]

CARLETON RODE CB 1857 [Mfc 73216]; M 1560-1812 [59]; M(I) 1560-1812 [Boyd]

CARLETON ST PETER see CARLTON NEXT LANGLEY

CARLTON NEXT LANGLEY C Ext 1562-1643 1659-1812 M Ext 1564-1643 1659-1746 B Ext 1566-1643 1659-1797 [Mf 1043]

CASTLE ACRE M 1600-1707 [60]; M 1710-1813 [AS]; M(I) 1601-1813 [Boyd]

CASTLE RISING C 1573-1840 1856 M 1573-1642 1664 1707-1836 B 1605 1627-44 1707-1840 [72]; M 1573-1643 1707-1836 [64]; M(I) 1573-1837 [Boyd]

CASTON C 1539-1614 1622-1720 M 1541-1624 1635-38 1666 1677 1689-90 B 1539-1676 1687-1718 [Mf 991];

M 1539-1700 [10]; M 1539-1700 [90]; M(I) 1539-1700 [Boyd]

CATFIELD C 1559-1812 M 1559-1712 1723-1837 B 1559-1603 1611-1812 briefs 1660 [Mf 991]; M(I) 1559-1837 [Boyd]

CATTON, OLD St Margaret C 1688-1841 M 1695-1840 B 1691-1851 [111]; C 1688-1812 M 1695-1753 B 1691-1812 [Mf 1654]; M 1695-1743 [Mf 1093]

CHEDGRAVE C 1550-1661 1670-1812 M 1551-1842 B 1551-1812 [Mf 1093]; C Ext 1550-1805 M Ext 1551-1803 B Ext 1551-1810 [Mf 1043]; M 1551-53 1564-1812 [AS]; M 1561-1654 1673-79/80 1701-19 1730-53 [Mf 1044]; M(I) 1550-1812 [Boyd]

CLAXTON CB 1691/92 CMB 1713/14 1717/18 [Mf 987]; see also BURSTON

CLEY C 1539-1667 1686-1743 M 1560-1667 1687-1743 B 1558-1667 1686-1743 [Mf 1849]

COCKLEY CLEY CMB 1691-1837 1841-61 [49]

COCKTHORPE CB 1560-1812 M 1560-1834 1858-1902 banns 1823-54 [Mfc 66604]; CMB 1560-1812 [74]; CMB 1764-1811 [87]

COLBY CB 1553-1812 M 1553-1755 [Mf 1653]; CMB 1684-1812 [92]

COLNEY CMB 1705/6-1837 [85]; CMB 1746-47 [Mf 987]

COLTISHALL C 1558-1808 M 1558-1754 B 1558-1812 [74]; M(I) 1558-1744 [Boyd]

COLVESTON see DIDLINGTON

CONGHAM CB 1580-1812 M 1581-1812 banns 1754-1800 [Mf 613]; CB 1580-86 1591-1812 [92]; M 1552-1837 [64]; M(I) 1581-1837 [Boyd]

CORPUSTY CMB 1730-1812 [97]

COSTESSEY CB 1538-1812 M 1539-1812 [Mf 1652]

COSTESSEY Cossey Hall Rom Cath C 1769-70 1785-1821 M 1812-13 [RC/PER]

CRANWICH CMB 1691-1837 [49]; M(I) 1734-39 1751-53 [Boyd]

CREAKE, NORTH CB 1538-1840 M 1538-1841 [72]

CREAKE, SOUTH C 1538-1840 M

1550-1838 B 1538-1841 [9]; M 1550-1837[63]; M(I) 1550-1837 [Boyd]

CREAKE, SOUTH Ind chapel B 1795 1828 [Mfc 91250]

CRESSINGHAM, GREAT M 1557-1652 1658-1812 [AS]; M(I) 1557-1812 [Boyd]

CRESSINGHAM, LITTLE C 1691-1837 M 1692-1716 1725-28 1741-1836 B 1693-1732 1741-1837 [85]

CRIMPLESHAM CMB Ext 1561-1809 [Mf 1044]

CRINGLEFORD C 1561-1854 [Mf 1044]; CB 1561-1840 [83]; M 1561-1837 [60]; M(I) 1561-1837 [Boyd]

CROSTWICK M 1561-1753 [Mf 1044]; M(I) 1561-1753 [Boyd]

CROSTWIGHT All Saints C 1698-1812 M 1712-1836 B 1708-93 1801-12 [Mf 991]; M(I) 1712-1837 [Boyd]; CMB Ext 1696-1812 [Mf 1043]

CROWNTHORPE C 1700-1912 M 1700-1920 B 1701-1812 banns 1754-1872 [Mfc 66606]

CROXTON *see* FULMODESTONE

CROXTON M(I) 1564-1751 [Boyd]

DENTON St Mary the Virgin M(I) 1559-1753 [Boyd]

DENTON Ind Chapel B 1806-37 [Mfc 9124]

DEREHAM, EAST C 1679-1838 MB 1679-1837 [Mf 1656-1657] C(I) 1679-1836 M(I) 1679-1837 B(I) 1761-1838 [Mf 1658-1659]

DEREHAM, EAST Cemetery B(I) 1869-1921 (1924 unconsecrated ground) [M 21]

DEREHAM, WEST M 1558-1753 [Mf 1044]; M(I) 1558-1753 [Boyd]

DERSINGHAM C 1653-67 M 1653-1718 B 1618-87 [11]; M 1653-1837 [67]; M(I) 1653-1836 [Boyd]

DICKLEBURGH B 1903 [Mfc 92008]; M 1540-1754 [Mf 1044]; M(I) 1540-1754 [Boyd]

DIDLINGTON M 1730-52 [Mf 1044]; M(I) 1730-52 [Boyd]

DIDLINGTON with COLVESTON CMB 1691-1837 [49]

DILHAM C 1563-1813 M 1563-1839 B 1563-1812 [Mf 990]; C 1565-1882 M

1564-1829 B 1566-1812 [Mf 1044]; C Ext 1691-1810 M Ext 1759-1806 B Ext 1693-1811 [Mf 1095]; CB 1903 [Mfc 92008]; M(I) 1563-1837 [Boyd]

DISS C 1903 [Mfc 92008]; CMB 1551-1837 [PER]; M(I) 1572-1754 [Boyd]

DISS Part Bapt Z 1806-36 [80]

DISS Presb B 1797 1803-07 1812 1818 1823-36 [Mfc 91250]

DISS Wes Meth B 1803-11 [Mfc 91246]

DITCHINGHAM C 1559-1726 M 1640-1707 B 1559-1729 [Mf 1621]; M 1559-1812 [60]; M(I) 1559-1812 [Boyd]

DOCKING M(I) 1558-1837 [Boyd]

DOCKING with SOUTHMERE M 1558-1837 [67]

DOWNHAM MARKET C 1541-1726 M 1557-1726 B 1554-1726 [Mf 1655]

DOWNHAM MARKET Wes Meth ZC 1814-37 [80]

DUNHAM, GREAT M(I) 1538-1812 [Boyd]

DUNHAM MAGNA M 1538-1812 [AS]

DUNSTON CMB 1557-1837 [49]; M(I) 1552-1811 [Boyd]

DUNTON CUM DOUGHTON C 1725-40 1782-1812 M 1784-1809 B 1727-36 1785-1811 [107]; M 1784-1837 [63]

DUNTON M(I) 1784-1837 [Boyd]

EARLHAM CMB 1621-1837 [85]

EARLHAM St Mary C 1621 1635-1746 M 1634-1754 B 1639-1748 [Mf 1661]; M(I) 1813-37 [PER]

EARSHAM M(I) 1559-1754 [Boyd]

EAST DEREHAM *see* MATTISHALL

EASTON C 1679-1903 M 1682-1834 banns 1824-1902 B 1678-1812 [Mfc 83090]

EATON C 1577-1812 M 1558-1698 1722-1812 B 1558-1660 1722-1812 [Mf 1662]

EATON St Andrew M(I) 1813-37 [PER]

ECCLES CB 1538-1704 M 1538-1704 [Mf 1660]; *see also* HEMPSTEAD

EDGEFIELD CMB 1730-1812 [92]

ELLINGHAM BY LODDON C 1671-1755 1787-1806 M 1588-1658 1722-32 1778 1810 B 1557-59 1594-1640 1679-1712 1733-37 1774-1809 [Mf 1043]

ELLINGHAM, GREAT B 1817-37 [Mfc 91247]

ELMHAM, NORTH C 1538-1858 M 1538-1837 B 1538-1934 [Mf 2851]; CMB 1538-1631 CMB Ext to 1791 [19]; CMB Ext 1538-1775 [20]; M(I) 1538-1631 [Boyd]

EMNETH C 1681-1949 M 1681-1968 B 1751-1920 [Mf 2374-75]

ERPINGHAM M(I) 1755-1837 [91]

FAKENHAM C 1719-1901 M 1719-88 1804-1901 B 1720-1910 [Mfc 66607]; M 1719-1837 [61]; M(I) 1719-1837 [Boyd]

FAKENHAM Prim Meth C Ext 1835-38 [83]

FELBRIGG C 1568-1812 MB 1556-1812 [Mf 1663]; CB 1725-1812 M 1731-1811 [86]

FELMINGHAM C 1725-1812 M 1725-57 1785-1811 B 1725-1811 [97]

FELTHORPE CB 1723-1812 M 1753-1812 [Mf 1852]

FELTWELL CB 1903 [Mfc 92008]

FERSFIELD CB 1565-1735 M 1565-1732 [Mf 1861]; M(I) 1565-1754 [Boyd]

FILBY CMB 1561-1812 [Mf 1047]; M 1561-1837 [62]; M(I) 1561-1837 [Boyd]

FINCHAM St Martin M 1543-1812 [47]

FINCHAM St Michael M 1587-1649 1661-1745 [47]

FLITCHAM M 1755-1837 [64]; M(I) 1755-1837 [Boyd]

FLORDON CMB 1558-1724 [Mf 1664]

FORDHAM C 1563-1729 1786-91 1796 MB 1577-1729 B 1785-91 [Mf 1665]; CMB 1576-1837 [49]

FORNCETT St Mary CMB 1688-1812 [GCI]

FORNCETT St Peter CMB 1561-1837 [GCI]

FOULDEN M(I) 1539-1753 [Boyd]

FOULSHAM B 1823-25 [Mfc 91247]; M 1559-1686 [Mf 1095]; M 1713-70 [Mf 2406]

FRAMINGHAM EARL CMB 1707-17/18 [Mf 987]; M(I) 1721-53 [Boyd]

FRAMINGHAM PIGOT M(I) 1553-1728 [Boyd]

FRAMINGHAM PIGOT Part Bapt Z 1808-36 [80]

FRANSHAM, GREAT CMB Ext 1559-1811 [20]

FRANSHAM, LITTLE CMB Ext 1538-1737 [20]

FRENZE C 1654-1830 1852 M 1662-1852 B 1651-1877 [49]; M(I) 1662-1753 [Boyd]

FRETTENHAM C 1801-02 B 1785-1809 [Mf 1666]; C 1813-81 M 1813-36 Banns 1824-86 [113]

FRING CB 1903 [Mfc 92008]; M 1700-1812 [60]; M(I) 1700-1812 [Boyd]

FRITTON CMB 1558-1728 [7]

FULMODESTONE with CROXTON C 1727-28 1741-42 1753-1812 M 1728 1753-1812 B 1727-28 1741 1753-1812 [107]

GARBOLDISHAM C 1609-1715 1723-1838 M 1609-1715 1723-1837 B 1609-1712 1723-1839 [Mf 1667]; C 1813-47 M 1813-37 B 1813-81 [87]

GARVESTON C 1813-61 M 1813-37 B 1813-1900 [107]

GASTHORPE M(I) 1729-42 [Boyd]

GATELEY CMB 1682-1812 [Mf 1668]

GAYTON M 1702-1837 [65]; M(I) 1702-1837 [Boyd]

GAYTON THORPE M 1575-1837 [65]; M(I) 1575-1837 [Boyd]

GAYWOOD M 1653-1837 [64]; M(I) 1653-1837 [Boyd]

GIMINGHAM C 1565-1695 1705-1812 M 1558-1695 1705-1845 B 1558-1686 1704-1812 [Mf 990]; C Ext 1566-1684 1706-1812 M Ext 1558-1695 1705-1835 B Ext 1558-1686 1704-1812 [Mf 1087]; CMB 1725-1811 [89]; M(I) 1558-1837 [Boyd]

GISSING C 1540-42 (illegible) 1563-1639 (gaps) 1684-1868 M 1563-1639 (gaps) 1705-1968 B 1539 1551 (illegible) 1563-1639 (gaps) 1702-1935 [Mf 3481B]; CMB 1691-99 1713-14 1739-40 1796 [Mf 987]; M(I) 1562-38 1705-53 [Boyd]

GLANDFORD CMB 1687-1812 [89]

GODWICK *see* TITTLESHALL

GOODERSTONE CMB 1563-1635 1702-1837 [85]

GRESHAM C 1559-1713 1732-83 M 1559-1713 1733-51 B 1559-1713 1733-83 [Mf 990]; C(I) 1634-1812 M(I) 1639-1774 B(I) 1639-1810 [110]; CMB 1725-27 1731 1735 1737-1812 [87]; M 1690-1812 [59]; M(I) 1690-1812 [Boyd]

GRIMSTON M 1552-1837 [64]; M(I) 1552-1837 [Boyd]

GUIST B 1813-38 [Mf 1853]; C 1557-1877 M 1561-1706 1722-1836 B 1558-1812 [Mfc 70679]

GUNTHORPE C 1558-1910 M 1558-1654 1661-1900 B 1558-86 1606-1618 1660-1727 1733-1813 [Mfc 79862] *see also* BALE

GUNTHORPE St Mary C(I) 1558-1910 M(I) 1559-1949 B(I) 1558-1934 [92]

GUNTON C 1723-1927 M 1724-1832 1848-1908 banns 1759-1940 B 1723-1963 [Mfc 66598]; CMB 1732-1811 [90]

HACKFORD C 1584-1901 M 1559-1647 1660-1771 1813-1901 B 1559-1901 [Mfc 66608]

HADDISCOE St Mary C 1903 1908 B 1903 1905 1908 [Mfc 92008]

HADDISCOE THORPE *see* THORPE NEXT HADDISCOE

HALES C 1906-08 B 1906-07 [Mfc 92008]; C 1674-1719 1733-1874 M 1704-1871 B 1678-1874; [Mf 2822]

HALVERGATE CB 1550-1784 (gaps) M 1550-1760 (gaps) [Mf 1669]

HANWORTH CMB 1727-1812 [89]

HAPPISBURGH C 1558-1812 M 1558-1655 1664-1729 1737-1837 B 1558-1719 1737-37 1749 1758-1812 [Mf 990]; M(I) 1558-1837 [Boyd]

HAPTON Presb B 1808-09 1827-34 Ind [Mfc 91250]

HAPTON Unit ZCB 1792-1834 [80]

HARDLEY CB 1903-05 1908 [Mfc 92008]; CMB 1708-09 1713-14 [Mf 987]

HARDWICK CB 1561-1812 M 1561-1795 [Mf 1671]

HARGHAM CM 1501-1741 B 1661 1740 [Mf 1672]

HARLING, EAST CB 1903-05 1908 [Mfc 92008]; C 1544-1730 M 1544-

1725 B 1544-1727 [Mf 1673]

HARLING, WEST CM 1539-1721 1728 C 1788-1812 M 1759-1906 B 1539-1812 [Mfc 66609]; CMB 1538-1598 [Mf 1670]

HAVERINGLAND CMB 1600-1754 1694-1837 [85]

HEACHAM CB 1903-07 [Mfc 92008]; M 1558-1643 1692-1812 [AS]; M(I) 1558-1812 [Boyd]

HECKINGHAM C 1812 1905-08 M 1812 B 1812 1906-08 [Mfc 92008]; C 1560-1662 1686 1695 1700-1873 M 1560-1641 1702-1871 B 1559-1875 [Mf 2822]; M(I) 1559-1812 [Boyd]

HEDENHAM CMB 1812 [Mfc 92008]; M 1559-1812 [59]; M(I) 1559-1812 [Boyd]

HEIGHAM C 1812 1852 M 1812 B 1812 1852 1854 [Mfc 92008]

HEIGHAM St Bartholomew CB 1538-1840 M 1538-1837 [Mfc 90941] M(I) 1813-37 [PER]

HELHOUGHTON C 1539-1921 M 1539-1900 B 1539-1905 [Mfc 66610]; M 1539-1650 1660-1836 [63]; M(I) 1539-1837 [Boyd]

HELLINGTON CMB 1812 CB 1835-39 [Mfc 92008]; CMB 1562-1812 [Mf 1674]

HEMBLINGTON C 1563-1869 M 1568-1833 B Ext 1664-1877 [Mf 1046]; M 1564-1812 [AS]; M(I) 1564-1812 [Boyd]

HEMPNALL formerly **Hemenhall**

HEMPNALL C 1812 1839 1841 1845 1852 1854 1868 1873 M 1812 B 1812 1839 1841 1845 1847 1852 1854 1868 1873 [Mfc 92008]; C 1568-98 1613-90 1703-27 1743 M 1560-97 1613-42 1654-1731 B 1560-98 1613-41 1662-1734 [Mf 1675]

HEMPNALL St Margaret C 1567-98 1613-1908 M 1561-97 1613-42 1654-91 1703-1904 B 1560-98 1613-42 1658 1662-1902 1770-71 1793 1746-68 [Mfc 89367]

HEMPSTEAD BY HOLT C 1558-1839 M 1558-1835 B 1558-1812 [Mf 1678]; CMB 1730-1812 [89]

HEMPSTEAD M(I) 1707-1837 [Boyd]

HEMPSTEAD with ECCLES CMB 1812

1824 CB 1845 1852 1854 1865-68 [Mfc 92008]; Z 1806-13 C 1707-1813 M 1707-1837 B 1707-1812 [Mf 992]

HEMSBY CMB 1556-1812 banns 1815-23 [Mf 988]; M 1556-1837 [62]; M(I) 1556-1837 [Boyd]

HETHEL CMB 1812-13 1824 CB 1839 1841 1843-47 1852 1854 1873 [Mfc 92008]

HETHERSETT C 1812-13 1821 1824 1839 1841 1845 1847 1852-54 1857 M 1812-13 1821 1824 B 1812-13 1819 1821 1824 1839 1841 1845 1847 1852 1854 1857 [Mfc 92008]; C 1617-55 1694-1838 M 1620-52 1695-1837 B 1617-50? 1696-1837 [Mf 1639]

HEVINGHAM C 1600-08 1628-33 1648-1839 M 1601-08 1628-33 1654-1836 B 1600-08 1628-33 1654-1837 [44]

HICKLING C 1812-13 1819-22 1824 1839 1841 1845 1847-48 1852-53 1856-57 1863-71 M 1812-13 1817 1819-22 1824 B 1812-13 1817 1819-22 1824 1839 1841 1845 1847-48 1852-53 1856-57 [Mfc 92008]; C 1653-1716 MB 1564-1716 [Mf 1098]; M 1657-1812 [59]; M(I) 1657-1812 [Boyd]

HILBOROUGH CMB 1813 1815 1817 1819-22 1824 CB 1839 1841 1845 1847-48 1852-54 1857 1867-68 1871 1873 [Mfc 92008]

HILDERSTONE *see* HINDOLVERSTON

HILGAY C 1812-13 1815 1817 1819-22 1829 1831 1843-50 1852-54 1857 1866-68 1871 M 1812-15 1817 1819-22 1829 1831-32 1842 B 1812-15 1817 1819-22 1826 1829 1831-32 1842-50 1852-54 1857 1866-68 1871 [Mfc 92008]; M 1583-1760 [Mf 1098]; M(I) 1583-1760 [Boyd]

HILLINGTON CB 1840-41 1853 [Mfc 92008]; M 1695-1837 [64]; M(I) 1695-1837 [Boyd]

HINDOLVERSTON alias **HILDERSTONE** C 1693-1730 1738-84 M 1722-27 1739-47 B 1722-27 1738-45 1770 1777-84 [24]

HINGHAM CMB 1812-17 1819-22 1824 C 1826-27 1829 1831-33 1839-48

1850-54 1857 1864-68 1871 1873 M 1826-27 1829 1831-33 B 1826-29 1831-33 1839-48 1850-54 1857-58 1864-68 1871 1873 [Mfc 92008]; C 1600-66 1683-1912 M 1600-64 1683-1812 1828-1903 banns 1754-1910 B 1600-52 1683-1906 [Mfc 66602]; CMB 1600-45 [90];**M** M(I) 1600-45 [Boyd]

HOCKERING C 1561-1781 B 1561-1728 M 1561-1735 [Mf 1676]; M(I) 1561-1754 [Boyd]

HOCKERING with MATTISHALL BURGH CMB 1812-21 1824 1826-33 1837 C 1842 1850-57 1864-65 1867-68 B 1842-57 1864-65 1867-68 [Mfc 92008]

HOCKHAM C 1812-33 1836-44 1846-48 1850-55 M 1812-24 1826-33 1837 B 1812-33 1836-44 1846-48 1850-55 [Mfc 92008]

HOCKHAM, GREAT with LITTLE C 1723-1856 M 1721-1837 B 1721-1870 [107]

HOCKWOLD with WILTON CB 1812-34 1836-73 1903-05 1907-08 M 1812-34 1836-37 [Mfc 92008]; C 1640 1644 1648-53 1655-57 1660-62 1663-1789 M 1662-1754 B 1658-1789 [Mf 3594]; CMB 1725-1812 (gaps) [Mfc 92000]

HOCKWOLD M 1662-1837 [90]; M(I) 1662-1837 [Boyd]

HOLKHAM M 1542-45 1560-1812 [AS]; M(I) 1542-1812 [Boyd]

HOLME BY THE SEA M 1705-1812 [60]; M(I) 1704-1811 [Boyd]

HOLME HALE C 1812-33 1836-41 1843-58 1864 1866-68 1870-71 1873 M 1812-33 1836-37 B 1812-18 1820-33 1836-58 1864 1866-68 1870-71 1873 [Mfc 92008]; M 1539-1837 [60]; M(I) 1539-1837 [Boyd]

HOLME NEXT THE SEA CMB 1813-16 1818 1820-23 C 1825-28 1830-33 1836-41 1843-45 1847-58 1864-65 1867-68 1873 1894-97 1901-07 M 1825-28 1830-33 1836-37 B 1825-33 1836-41 1843-45 1847-51 1853-58 1864-65 1867-68 1873 1894-97 1901-07 [Mfc 92008]; CB 1704-1812 M 1705-1784 [Mf 1047]

HOLT MARKET CMB Ext 1557-1605 1676-95 [Mf 1098]

15

HONING C 1813-16 1818 1821-23 1825-33 1836-40 1843-51 1854-56 1858 1863-71 1873 1903-05 1907-08 M 1813-16 1818 1821 1823 1825-30 1832-33 1836-37 B 1813-14 1816 1818 1821 1823 1825-33 1836-40 1843-46 1848-51 1854-56 1858 1863-71 1873 1903-05 1907-08 [Mfc 92008]; C Ext 1630-1813 M Ext 1653-1812 B Ext 1654-1813 [Mf 1098]; CB 1630-1813 M 1630-1836 [Mf 992]; M(I) 1630-1836 [Boyd]

HONINGHAM CMB 1813-14 1818 1821 1823 1825-30 1832-33 C 1836-40 1843-44 1846 1848 1851 1854-55 1858 1864-68 1871 1873 M 1836-37 1839-40 B 1836-40 1843-44 1846 1848 1851 1855 1858 1864-68 1871 1873 [Mfc 92008]; C 1563-1726 M 1563-1633 1664-74 1711 1717 1723 B 1563-1633 1724-27 [Mf 1683]

HORNHILL see HORNING

HORNING alias **HORNHILL** CMB 1813 1816 1818 1821 1823 1825 C 1827-28 1830 1832-33 1836-40 1843-44 1846 1851 1855 1858 1864 1871 1900-05 M 1828 1830 1836-40 1843-44 1846 1851 B 1828 1830 1836-40 1843-44 1846 1851 1855 1858 1864 1871 1900-05 [Mfc 92008]; CB Ext 1558-1837 Ext M 1558-1754 [Mf 1098]; M(I) 1558-1754 [Boyd]

HORNING BY LINDHAM C 1559-1827 M 1559-1686 1701-54 1813-37 B 1559-1877 [Mf 1095]

HORNINGTOFT CMB Ext 1542-1757 [20]; M 1539-1837 [63]; M(I) 1539-1837 [Boyd]

HORSEY CMB 1813 1816 1818 1821 1823 1825 1828 1830 C 1836-40 1843-44 1846 1851 1855-56 1858 1864-68 M 1836-37 1840 B 1836-40 1843-44 1846 1851 1855-56 1858 1864-67 [Mfc 92008]; C 1559-1646 1666-1812 M 1572-1637 1659-66 1677 1758-1824 B 1559-1647 1665-1811 [Mf 992]; C Ext 1559-1870 M Ext 1571-1770 B Ext 1559-1813 [Mf 1097]; C Ext 1813-70 M Ext 1755-1812 B Ext 1813-68 [Mf 1095]; C 1813-1964 [91]

HORSFORD All Saints C 1597-98

1606-1972 M 1598 1607-43 1652-57 1662-1735 1739-50 1754-1962 M(I) 1813-1913 B 1597-98 1607-44 1650-57 1662-1952 banns 1824-1966 confirmations 1951-52 1955 1961 1964 [Mf 3614-3615]

HORSTEAD M 1558-1648 1654 1661-1811 [AS]; M(I) 1558-1812 [Boyd]

HOUGHTON NEXT HARPLEY CMB 1813 1816 1818 1821 1823 1825 1830 1836-37 CB 1844 1846 1856 1858 1864 1871 [Mfc 92008]; C 1654-1905 M 1654-1740 1756-1903 banns 1755-1810 1849-1901 B 1654-1812 [Mfc 66613]

HOUGHTON ON THE HILL CMB 1813 1816 1818 1821 1823 1825 C 1830 1836 1843 1851 M 1836 B 1830 1836 1843 1851 [Mfc 92008]

HOUGHTON St Giles C 1559-1875 M 1559-1902 B 1559-1762 1783-1812 [Mfc 66599]; C 1729/30-1812 M 1729-1811 B 1729-1812 [97]

HOVETON St John CMB 1813 1816 1821 1823 1825 C 1836-40 1843-44 1846 1868-71 1873 M 1836-37 B 1836-39 1843 1846 1868-71 1873 [Mfc 92008]; C 1673-1726 1812 M 1674-1728 B 1673-1733 [Mf 1630]; C 1673-1914 M 1673-1903 B 1673-1904 [Mfc 66614]

HOVETON St Peter CMB 1813 1816 1821 1823 1825 C 1836-39 1844 1846 1858-60 1868-71 M 1836-37 B 1836-39 1846 1868-71 [Mfc 92008]; C 1624-1905 M 1624-1903 banns 1755-1914 B 1625-1812 [Mfc 66615]; CMB 1624-1728 [Mf 1629]

HOWE CMB 1708-09 1717-18 [Mf 987]; M(I) 1607-1812 [Boyd]

HOWE with WEST (LITTLE) PORINGLAND CMB 1813 1821 1823 C 1851 1865-1907 B 1851 1865-92 1906-07 [Mfc 92008]

HUNSTANTON C 1538-1730 M 1542-1721 B 1538-1810 [83]

HUNSTANTON with RINGSTEAD PARVA CMB 1813 1821 C 1823 1825 1836-39 1846 1856 1858 1865-66 1871 1901-08 M 1825 1836 B 1836 1838-39 1846 1856 1858 1865-66 1871 1901-05 [Mfc 92008]

HUNWORTH CMB 1729-1812 [90]
ICKBURGH C 1813 1821 1838 1846
1856 1858 1865 1870-71 M 1821 B
1813 1821 1838 1856 1858 1865
1870-71 [Mfc 92008]
ICKBURGH CMB 1693-1709 1716-47
1753 1725/26-68 (ATs) C 1769-1812
M 1773-1836 banns 1773-1812 B
1769-1836 [85]
ILLINGTON CMB 1821 1836 C 1838
1865-71 B 1838 1865-69 [Mfc 92008];
C 1672-1770 1783-1812 M 1673-1843
banns 1851-1913 B 1675-1772 1783-
1812 [Mfc 66616]
INGHAM B 1785-1821 Bapt [Mfc
91247]; C 1836 CM 1838 1854-56
[Mfc 92008]; C 1800-12 M 1801-38 B
1801-12 [Mf 992]; C 1698 1705-28
1734-1812 M 1705-09 1715-24 1734-
1838 B 1698 1705-29 1734-1812
banns 1803 1814 1824-29 1835-39
[113]; CMB 1713-14 1716-17 1736-36
1739-40 1744-45 1747-48 1752-53
1796-97 [Mf 987]; M(I) 1801-38 [Boyd]
INGOLDISTHORPE CM 1739-40 [Mf
987]; M 1754-1837 [67]; CB 1838
1856 1858 1865 1903-04 1906-07
[Mfc 92008]; M(I) 1754-1837 [Boyd]
INGWORTH M 1559-1812 [AS]; M(I)
1558-1812 [Boyd]
INTWOOD C 1538-1726 M 1698-1726
B 1558-1724 [Mf 1677]
INTWOOD with KESWICK CB 1858
1865 [Mfc 92008]
IRSTEAD C 1856 1865 B 1856 1858
1865 [Mfc 92008]; CMB 1538-1733
[Mf 1631]
ITTERINGHAM CB 1717-1812 M 1720-
1811 [97]
KENNINGHALL CB 1856 1865 [Mfc
92008]
KENNINGHALL C 1558-1727 M 1558-
1724 B 1558-1717 [Mf 1681]
KESWICK see INTWOOD
KETTERINGHAM CMB 1695-1733 [Mf
1682]
KETTLESTONE CB 1856 [Mfc 92008];
C 1725-1811 M 1725-1812 B 1725-
1812 [97]
KIMBERLEY CB 1856 [Mfc 92008];
CMB 1739-40 [Mf 987]
KINGS LYNN Broad Street Ind C c.

1745-49 at Maidenhead [83]
KINGS LYNN C(I) 1771-94 [113]
KINGS LYNN St Margaret C 1559-
1692 1721-1838 M 1559-1653 1722-
54 1777-1837 B 1559-1838 [Mf 1622-
1624]; C 1559-1776 M 1559-1777 B
1559-1722 [Mf 2736]; C 1653-58
1693-1720 M 1563-1722 B 1653-1720
[Mf 1848]
KINGS LYNN St Nicholas C 1628-
1738 M 1562-1738 1754-1837 B
1562-1841 [Mf 1625-1626]; C 1628-
1812 1843-1931 M 1562-1754 B
1562-1680 [Mf 2684-5]
KINGS LYNN Stepney Part Bapt B
1843-57 [Mfc 91247]
KIRBY BEDON CB 1856 [Mfc 92008];
M(I) 1568-1753 [Boyd]
KIRBY CANE CB 1856 [Mfc 92008]
KNAPTON C 1901-02 [Mfc 92008]; C
1687-1813 M 1687-1836 B 1687-1812
1711-12 [Mf 992]; C 1692-1812 MB
1687-1812 banns 1757-1834 [Mf
1095]; M(I) 1687-1837 [Boyd]
LAKENHAM C 1856 [Mfc 92008]; C
1605-1813 M 1601-49 1662-1812 B
1572-74 1602-1808 [Mf 1684]
LAKENHAM, OLD M(I) 1801-37 [73]
LAKENHAM St John C 1601-1901 M
1568-74 1602-44 1664-1901 B 1568-
74 1602-1902 [Mfc 66618]
LAKENHAM St John the Bapt & All
Saints M(I) 1813-37 [PER]
LAKENHEATH Prim Meth B 1831-37
[Mfc 91246]
LAMMAS & LITTLE HAUTBOIS C
1539-1705 M 1539-1707 1718-83 B
1538-1723 CMB Ext 1723-1894 [21]
LAMMAS M(I) 1539-1723 [Boyd]
LAMMAS SFrs M(I) 1813-37 [PER]
LANGFORD CB 1856 [Mfc 92008];
CMB 1692-1705 1717; [85]
LANGHAM BISHOPS M(I) 1710-1812
[Boyd]
LANGHAM C 1695-1880 M 1710-1837
banns 1755-1812 B 1695-1812 [Mfc
67240]
LANGHAM Episc M 1710-44 1755-
1812 [AS]
LANGLEY M 1695-1812 [AS]; M(I)
1701-1812 [Boyd]

LARLING C 1723-1812 M 1723-1839
banns 1824-1903 B 1678-83 1723-
1812 [Mfc 67294]

LESSINGHAM C 1557-1812 M 1557-
1837 B 1557-1811 [Mf 992]; M(I)
1557-1837 [Boyd]

LETHERINGSETT CMB 1601-08 1623-
36 C 1653-1759 M 1662-1752 B
1653-1760 [Mf 992]; CMB 1714-1812
[89]; M(I) 1662-1752 [Boyd]

LEXHAM, EAST M 1541-1812 [AS];
M(I) 1541-1812 [Boyd]

LIMPENHOE Z 1763-66 CM 1662-1793
banns 1763-1810 B 1662-1790 [Mf
1851]

LINGWOOD C 1561-1838 M 1562-1757
(gaps) B 1561-1813 [Mf 1685]; CMB
1561-1817 [Mf 1047]

LITCHAM CMB Ext 1550-1710 [20]; M
1555-1645 1651-1812 [AS]; M(I)
1555-1812 [Boyd]

LONGHAM CMB Ext 1564-1761 [20]

LONGHAM St Andrew C 1560-1900 M
1560-1670 1676-1734 1743-1900 B
1561-1900 Banns 1758 1764-71
1779-84 1794-1811 [26]

LOPHAM, NORTH M(I) 1561-1753
[Boyd]

LOPHAM, SOUTH M(I) 1561-1753
[Boyd]

LUDHAM CMB Ext 1582-1853 [Mf 993];
CB 1903-04 [Mfc 92008]

LYNN WEST St Peter C 1736-1838 M
1695-1837 B 1715-1838 [Mf 1686]

MARHAM C 1562-1730 CMB Ext 1539-
1837 [Mf 993]

MARSHAM CMB 1538-1836 [69]; M(I)
1538-1837 [Boyd]

MARTHAM M(I) 1559-1838 [Boyd]

MASSINGHAM, GREAT M 1564-1837
[65]; M(I) 1564-1837 [Boyd]

MASSINGHAM, LITTLE M 1559-1837
[63]; M(I) 1539-1837 [Boyd]

MATLASKE CB 1558-1726 M 1558-
1723 [Mf 1687]; CMB 1725-1812 [90]

MATTISHALL BURGH see
HOCKFRING

MATTISHALL & EAST DEREHAM
Cong ZC 1772-1837 [80]

MATTISHALL & WATTON (Prim Meth)
ZC 1832-37 [80]

MATTISHALL Cong ZC 1772-85 1828-
37 [80]

MATTISHALL M(I) 1653-1753 [Boyd]

MAUTBY CB 1664-1802 M 1663-1730
1758-34 [Mfc 67241]; CMB 1600-36
1663-1802 M 1813-34 [Mf 1047]; M
1663-1834 [60]; M(I) 1663-1834
[Boyd]

MELTON, LITTLE CMB 1724-25 [Mf
987]; CMB 1734-1837 [85]

METHWOLD CMB 1683-1726 [Mf
1708]

METTON C 1725 1731-1812 M 1738-
1803 B 1731-1811 [86]; C 1738-70 M
1738-54 B 1738-1812 [Mf 1620]

MIDDLETON M 1560-1839 [65]; M(I)
1560-1837 [Boyd]

MILEHAM CMB Ext 1569-1787 [20];
M(I) 1540-1753 [Boyd]

MORNINGTHORPE C 1557-1727 MB
1562-1727 [Mf 1691]

MORSTON C 1700-1811 1837-42 M
1701-1915 B 1700-1812 banns 1933-
35 [Mfc 67242]; CB 1689-1811 M
1689-1810 [87]

MORTON ON THE HILL CB 1559-1812
M 1561-1837 banns 1824-1906 [Mfc
67243]

MOULTON ST MARY C 1539-1902 M
1539-1654 1663-1723 1739-1903
banns 1824-1912 B 1539-1725 1735-
1906 [Mfc 67244]; M(I) 1531-1752
[Boyd]

MULBARTON M(I) 1547-1732 [Boyd]

MUNDESLEY C 1756-1801 M 1726-44
B 1756-1812 [Mf 1043]; CMB 1724-25
[Mf 987]; M 1725-1812 [AS]; M(I)
1726-1812 [Boyd]

MUNDFORD CB 1699-1739 M 1699-
1720 1731/2-38 [83]; M(I) 1700-54
[Boyd]

MUNDHAM M(I) 1559-1812 [Boyd]

NARBOROUGH M 1558-1812 [AS];
M(I) 1558-1812 [Boyd]

NARFORD M 1599-1650 1667-1752
1783-1811 [AS]; M(I) 1599-1811
[Boyd]

NEATISHEAD C 1903-04 [Mfc 92008];
CMB 1676-1727 [Mf 1627]

NEATISHEAD Part Bapt CB 1801-37
[Mfc 91245]

NECTON CMB Ext 1558-1678 [20];
CMB 1558-1812 [Mf 1690]
NEEDHAM M 1644-77 1696-1750 [Mf
1044]; M(I) 1644-1750 [Boyd]
NEWTON BY CASTLEACRE St Mary
C 1559-86 1598-1681 1692-1813
1822 M 1561-82 1613-15 1626 1636-
55 1669 1693-98 1705 1712-24 B
1559-86 1599-1725 1733-36 1743-99
[31]; CMB 1752-53 [Mf 987]; M(I)
1561-1724 [Boyd]
NEWTON FLOTMAN M(I) 1558-1753
[Boyd]
NEWTON, WEST M 1561-1837 [60];
M(I) 1561-1837 [Boyd]
NORTHWOLD CM 1656-86 1695-1727
B 1656-85 1695-1827 [Mf 1689]
NORTON SUBCOURSE C 1560-1873
M 1560-1811 1813-71 B 1560-1872
[Mf 2822-3]
NORWICH M(I) 1813-37 [PER]
NORWICH All Saints M(I) 1813-37
[PER]
NORWICH Cathedral C 1702-1811 M
1697-1754 B 1703-1812 [Mf 1091];
C(I) 1702-1811 [Mf 1419]; M 1697-
1754 [35]; M(I) 1697-1754 [Boyd]
NORWICH St Andrew M(I) 1813-37
[PER]
NORWICH St Augustine C 1558-1859
M 1558-1812 B 1558-1838 [Mf 1692];
M(I) 1813-37 [PER]
NORWICH St Benedict C 1586-1840 M
1562-1837 B 1563-1840 1855 1872;
[93-94]; M(I) 1813-37 [PER]
NORWICH St Clement M(I) 1813-37
[PER]
NORWICH St Edmund M(I) 1813-37
[PER]
NORWICH St Etheldreda M(I) 1813-37
[PER]
NORWICH St George Colegate C
1538-1838 MB 1538-1837 [Mf 1688];
M(I) 1813-37 [PER]; M(I) 1813-37 [83]
NORWICH St George M(I) 1538-1707
[Boyd]
NORWICH St George Tombland C
1538-1707 M 1538-1642 1662-
1706/07 B 1559-1642 1662-1707 [30];
M(I) 1813-37 [PER]; Z 1740-1838 C
1707-1838 M 1702-1837 B 1703-

1854; MIs 1760-1855 [29]
NORWICH St Giles C 1538-1840 M
1540-1837 B 1538-1841 D 1837-41
1593 [4]; M(I) 1813-37 [PER]
NORWICH St Gregory M(I) 1813-37
[PER]
NORWICH St Helen & chapel of the
Great Hospital C 1708-40 1749-1841
M 1708-1836 B 1678-1739 1748-1856
[5]
NORWICH St Helen M(I) 1813-37
[PER]
NORWICH St James M(I) 1813-37
[PER]
NORWICH St James with Pockthorpe
Z 1652-54 1695-1706 1737-1840 C
1556-1841 M 1556-1837 B 1556-1856
[2-3]
NORWICH St John Maddermarket
M(I) 1813-37 [PER]
NORWICH St John Sepulchre M(I)
1813-37 [PER]
NORWICH St John Timberhill M(I)
1813-37 [PER]
NORWICH St Julian M(I) 1813-37
[PER]
NORWICH St Lawrence M(I) 1813-37
[PER]
NORWICH St Margaret C 1560-1840 M
1559-1837 B 1560-1840 [38-39]; M(I)
1813-37 [PER]
NORWICH St Martin at Oak C 1560-98
c. 1650-1848 1866-73 M 1628-38 c.
1640 - c. 1643 c. 1654 1659-1837 B
1666-1843 [40-42]; M(I) 1813-37
[PER]
NORWICH St Martin at Palace M
1538-1837 B 1538-1838; [36-37]; M(I)
1813-37 [PER]
NORWICH St Mary Coslany C 1813-53
1893 MB 1813-37 [34]; M 1557-86
1592-1812 [AS]; M(I) 1557-1812
[Boyd]; M(I) 1813-37 [PER]
NORWICH St Mary in the Marsh M(I)
1558-1812 [Boyd]; M(I) 1813-37 [PER]
NORWICH St Michael at Plea C 1538-
1695 M 1539-1695 B 1538-1691 [46];
CMB 1538-1695/96 [Mf 1091]; M(I)
1539-1700 [Boyd]; M(I) 1813-37 [PER]
NORWICH St Michael at Thorn M(I)
1813-37 [PER]

NORWICH St Michael Coslany CB 1558-1653 M 1558-1634 1649-52 1659-1837 [Mf 1091]; M(I) 1813-37 [PER]

NORWICH St Paul M(I) 1813-37 [PER]

NORWICH St Peter Hungate M 1602-1812 [110]; M(I) 1813-37 [PER]

NORWICH St Peter Mancroft M 1538-1738 [91]; M(I) 1813-37 [PER]

NORWICH St Peter per Mountergate C 1538-1901 M 1538-1904 B 1538-1870 1883 banns 1754-1901 [Mfc 85306]; M(I) 1813-37 [PER]

NORWICH St Peter Southgate M(I) 1813-37 [PER]

NORWICH St Saviour C 1555-1647 1655-1856 M 1555-1642 1652 1660-1837 B 1556-1840 [43]; M(I) 1813-37 [PER]

NORWICH St Simon & St Jude Z 1803-26 1847-64 C 1539-1840 1847-64 M 1539-1641 1658-1837 B 1539-1856 [1]; M(I) 1813-37 [PER]

NORWICH St Stephen C 1538-1904 M 1538-1892 B 1538-1867 1869 1874 banns 1754-1901 [Mfc 90958]; M(I) 1538-1722 [Boyd]; M(I) 1813-37 [PER]

NORWICH St Swithin M(I) 1813-37 [PER]

NORWICH Octagon Presb B 1759-1826 [Mfc 91250]

NORWICH Old Meeting House B 1751-1837 [Mfc 91241]; C 1657-81 [PER]

NORWICH Princes Street chapel B 1819-35 [Mfc 91250]

NORWICH SFrs M(I) 1813-37 [PER]

NORWICH Rosary cemetery B 1819-37 MIs 1819-1986 [PER]

NORWICH Tabernacle B 1753-58 1767 [Mfc 91246]

NORWICH Walloon C(I) 1595-1732 M(I) 1599-1611 CMB Ext 1579-1755 [HUG/PER]

OBY M 1563-1718 [62]; M(I) 1563-1718 [Boyd]

ORMESBY C(I) Ext 1570-1773 M(I) Ext 1591-1805 B(I) Ext 1578-1773 [Mf 994]

ORMESBY, GREAT C Ext 1667-1847 M Ext 1677-1837 B Ext 1677-1865 [Mf 994]

ORMESBY St Margaret M 1601-1837 [62]; M(I) 1601-1837 [Boyd]

ORMESBY St Michael M 1601-10 1623-28 1636 1669-1837 [62]; M(I) 1591-1837 [Boyd]

OVERSTRAND C 1725-1812 MB 1726-1811 [86]

OXBOROUGH M 1538-1743 [Mf 994]; M(I) 1538-1743 [Boyd]

OXNEAD CMB 1573-1731 1780-83 [Mf 1694]

PALLING C 1617-1711 1779-1812 M 1616-1711 B 1616-1711 1779-1812 [Mf 994]; C 1661-1701 1779-1993 M 1616-1701 1813-1994 B 1616-1701 1779-1812 [110]; C Ext 1779-1870 B Ext 1779-1811 1858-70 [Mf 1095]; M(I) 1616-76 [Boyd]

PANXWORTH C 1847-1913 M 1847-1902 B 1848-1910 [Mfc 67248]; M(I) 1561-1812 [Boyd]

PASTON CB 1904 [Mfc 92008]; CMB 1538-1631 1720-1812 [Mf 1047]; CMB Ext 1538-1812 [Mf 1043]

PENTNEY CB 1894 [Mfc 78023]; M 1731-1837 [65]; M(I) 1731-1837 [Boyd]

PLUMSTEAD BY HOLT C 1726/27-1811 M 1732-1811 B 1726/27-1812 [91]

PLUMSTEAD CMB 1559-1724 [Mf 1693]

PLUMSTEAD, GREAT C 1558-1807 M 1558-1752 B 1 Ext 561-1807 [Mf 1045]

PORINGLAND, WEST (LITTLE) see HOWE

POSTWICK CMB Ext 1570-1812 [Mf 1045]

POTTER HEIGHAM CMB(I) 1538-1812 [Mf 1045]

PULHAM St Mary M(I) 1539-1753 [Boyd]

PULHAM St Mary the Virgin & St Mary Magdalen B 1813-68 [97]

PULHAM St Mary the Virgin M 1539-1754 [Mf 1044]; C 1545-1733, M 1562-1689, B Ext 1544-1766 [NF/R 113]

QUIDENHAM CMB 1538-1725 [Mf

20

1695]

RACKHEATH CMB 1645-1837 [49]

RAINHAM, SOUTH or **RAYNHAM** M
1601-1837 [66]

RAINHAM St Martin CMB 1691-92
1708-09 [Mf 987]

RAINHAM, WEST or **RAYNHAM** M
1538-1764 [66]

RANWORTH C 1558-1915 M 1559-
1837 B 1559-1812 banns 1766-1816
1823-1908 [Mfc 67249]; C 1559-1795
M 1559-1765 B Ext 1558-1795 [Mf
1046]; M 1559-1643 1661-1745 1753-
1812 [AS]; M(I) 1559-1812 [Boyd]

RAYNHAM, EAST M(I) 1601-1837
[Boyd]

RAYNHAM, EAST or **RAYNHAM St
Mary** CB 1627-1716 [28]

RAYNHAM, SOUTH M(I) 1601-1837
[Boyd]

RAYNHAM, WEST C 1539-1653 1692
M 1538/39-1641 B 1538/39-1646
1662/63 [91]; M(I) 1538-1751 [Boyd]

REDENHALL CMB Ext 1558-1653 [Mf
1045]

REEDHAM CB Ext 1758-1837 M Ext
1754-1837 [Mf 1045]; CMB 1691-92
1708-09 [Mf 987]; M(I) 1558-1753
[Boyd]

REEPHAM with KERDISTON C 1538-
1723 1813-1903 M 1539-1714 1754-
1902 B 1539-1723 1813-63 [Mfc
66601]

REPPS CUM BASTWICK CB 1563-
1732 M Ext 1563-1733 [Mf 1096]; CB
1564-1802 M 1563-1811 [Mf 1096]

REPPS, NORTH CMB 1725-1811 [86]

REPPS, SOUTH CMB 1725-1812 [86]

RIDDLESWORTH M(I) 1688-1739
[Boyd]

RIDLINGTON C Ext 1559-1811 M Ext
1559-1810 B Ext 1563-1810 [Mf
1096]; C 1559-1812 M 1559-1643
1669-1838 B 1559-77 1590-1643
1653-1812 [Mf 992]; M(I) 1559-1837
[Boyd]

RINGSTEAD PARVA *see*
HUNSTANTON

ROCKLAND St Mary C 1539-1725 M
1539-1728 B 1539-1744 [Mf 1696]

ROCKLAND St Peter Prim Meth B

1837 [Mfc 91246]

ROLLESBY C(I) 1561-1812 M(I) 1559-
1812 B(I) 1564-1808 [Mf 1096]

ROUDHAM *see* BRIDGHAM

ROUDHAM C 1663-1739 1804-88 M
1663-1737 B 1663-1739 1803-1922
[Mfc 67250]

ROUGHAM CMB 1769-70 [Mf 987]

ROUGHTON B(I) 1813-1922 [96]; C(I)
1562-1812 M(I) 1563-1627 1711-1812
B(I) 1600-40 1678-1812 [45]; CMB
1562-1837 [17]; CMB 1725-1812 [87];
M(I) 1563-1837 [Boyd]

ROYDON CMB 1559-1837 [85]; CMB
1721-1835 [Mf 1096]; CMB 1721-1835
[73]; M 1721-1837 [64]

ROYDON NEAR DISS M(I) 1559-1753
[Boyd]

ROYDON NEAR LYNN C(I) 1721-1835
[Mf 1419]; M(I) 1721-1837 [Boyd]

RUDHAM, EAST M 1562-1837 [63];
M(I) 1562-1650 1726-1837 [Boyd]

RUDHAM, WEST M 1565-1837 [63];
M(I) 1565-1837 [Boyd]

RUNCTON HOLME CB 1901-03 [Mfc
92008]

RUNCTON, NORTH C 1563-1876 M
1563-1741 1754-1837 B 1563-1903
[Mfc 67251]; CB 1563-1652 M 1563-
1650 [51]; CB(I) 1563-1652 M(I) 1563-
1650 [83]; M 1563-1837 [66]; M(I)
1563-1837 [Boyd]

RUNHAM C 1539-1902 M 1539-1775
1785 1805-1901 B 1539-1812 [Mfc
67252]; C 1548-1790 M 1548-1772
banns 1805-11 B 1542-1790 [Mf
1092]; CB 1539-1812 M 1539-1785
1805 [Mf 1090]; M 1538-1812 [60];
M(I) 1539-1812 [Boyd]

RUNTON C 1744-1902 M 1744-54
1824-1924 banns 1754-1842 B 1743-
1902 [Mfc 67253]; M(I) 1754-1812 [97]

RUSHALL M 1562-1732 1754 [Mf
1044]; M(I) 1562-1754 [Boyd]

RUSHTON, EAST M(I) 1558-1837
[Boyd]

RUSHTON, SOUTH M(I) 1726-1835
[Boyd]

RUSTON, EAST C 1558-1901 M 1558-
1683 1693-1901 1824-1915 B 1558-
1889 [Mfc 67255]; CB 1559-1812 M
1559-1837 [Mf 995]; CMB 1558-1812

[Mf 1096]

RYBURGH, GREAT M(I) 1547-1837 [Boyd]

RYBURGH, GREAT St Andrew C 1547-1887 M 1547-1641 1650-1965 B 1547-1942 banns 1909-73 [112]

RYBURGH, LITTLE C 1688-1777 1785-1944 M 1695-1749 B 1697-1777 1786-1946 [97]; CMB 1725-1812 [112]; M(I) 1695-1749 [Boyd]

RYSTON CUM ROXTON CMB 1687-1837 [49]

SALLE C 1560-1812 M 1558-1753 B 1558-1812 [Mf 1698]

SANDRINGHAM M 1561-84 1595-1643 1653-54 1663-1812 [AS]; M(I) 1561-1812 [Boyd]

SANTON C 1903 [Mfc 92008]; CMB 1707-08 1769-1837 [49]; M(I) 1780-90 [Boyd]

SAXLINGHAM BY HOLT C 1558-1666 1709-1902 M 1558-1674 1683-95 1710-1905 banns 1754-1812 B 1558-1696 1708-1812 [Mfc 67256]

SAXLINGHAM CMB 1721-1812 [89]

SAXLINGHAM NETHERGATE & THORPE CMB 1556-1790 [Mf 1854]

SAXLINGHAM NETHERGATE M(I) 1558-1812 [Boyd]

SAXLINGHAM THORPE M(I) 1570-1739 [Boyd]

SAXLINGHAM THORPE Part Bapt Z 1793-1837 [80]

SAXTHORPE CB 1695-1791 M 1696-1754 [Mf 1855]; CB 1709-1805 M 1709-1802 [97]

SCARNING CMB Ext 1539-1778 [20]

SCO RUSTON C 1707-1812 M 1726-1835 B 1723-1812 [Mf 987]; C 1707-1837 M 1726-1837 B 1723-1837 [85]; C 1707-1902 M 1726-51 1758-1904 1911-13 banns 1777-1920 B 1723-1806 1814-1908 [Mfc 67257]

SCOLE M(I) 1563-1752 [Boyd]

SCULTHORPE CMB 1562-1726 [Mf 1699]; M 1561-1639 1651-1836 [61]; M(I) 1563-1837 [Boyd]

SEDGEFORD M 1560-1837 [67]; M(I) 1560-1837 [73]; M(I) 1560-1837 [Boyd]

SEETHING M(I) 1561-1812 [Boyd]

SHARRINGHAM Index to names [83]

SHARRINGTON CB 1672-1812 M 1673-1812 [Mf 1092]

SHELFANGER CMB 1686-1837 [85]; M(I) 1686-1837 [Boyd]

SHELFANGER (Part Bapt) Z 1795-1837 [80]

SHELTON CMB 1557-1653 C 1683-1812 M 1636-1812 B 1678-1795 [Mf 1697]

SHEREFORD C 1711-21 1727-48 1764-1810 M 1713 1727-38 1744 1749 1768-72 1778-1807 B 1710-21 1727-42 1748 1772-97 1802 1807-11 [107]; M 1772-1837 [63]; M(I) 1722-1837 [Boyd]

SHERINGHAM CMB 1670-1858 [At binding]; CMB(I) 1670-1858 [25]

SHERINGHAM All Saints M 1754-1812 [Mf 1090]

SHERNBORNE M 1755-1838 [67]; M(I) 1755-1837 [Boyd]

SHIMPLING M(I) 1538-1753 [Boyd]

SHINGHAM CMB 1691/92-1776/77 1762-1837 [49]; M 1762-1808 1822-36 banns 1798-1810 [Mf 1095]; M 1762-1836 [47]

SHIPDHAM CB 1558-1804 M 1558-1740 [Mf 1700]

SHIPDHAM Ind chapel C 1833-37 [86]

SHOTESHAM M(I) 1687-1775 [Boyd]

SHOTESHAM All Saints M 1561-1753 [Mf 1092]

SHOTESHAM St Mary CM 1687-1753 B 1687-1781 [Mf 1850]; M 1687-1753 [Mf 1092]

SHOULDHAM C 1653-54 1666-1725 MB 1665-1725 [Mf 2593]; M(I) 1561-1751 [Boyd]

SHROPHAM C 1721-1875 M 1721-1836 banns 1754-1902 B 1721-1918 [Mfc 67258]

SIDESTRAND CMB 1558-1858 [L 61 (missing 12/98)]; CMB 1725-1808 [86]

SIZELAND M(I) 1584-1812 [Boyd]

SLOLEY CMB 1560-1812 [Mf 1632]

SMALLBURGH CB 1561-1812 M 1561-1649 1663-1837 [Mf 995]

SNETTERTON C 1669-1932 M 1670-1812 1818-1913 B 1669-1812 [Mfc 67259]; CMB 1669-1729 [Mf 1720]

SNETTISHAM M 1682-1812 [AS]; M(I) 1682-1812 [Boyd]

SNORING, GREAT M(I) 1560-1837 [Boyd]

SNORING, LITTLE M(I) 1559-1837 [Boyd]

SNORING, MAGNA M 1563-1837 [61]

SNORING, PARVA M 1559-1615 1625-60 1664-1837 [61]

SOMERTON, EAST M(I) 1717-1837 [Boyd]; see also WINTERTON

SOMERTON, WEST C Ext 1736-1811 M Ext 1737-52 B Ext 1726-1812 [Mf 1043]; M 1737-1837 [62]; M(I) 1736-1837 [Boyd]

SOUTHACRE M 1576-1812 1 [AS]

SOUTHERY M(I) 1706-51 [Boyd]

SPIXWORTH M(I) 1554-1753 [Boyd]

SPROWSTON C 1690-1812 MB 1721-1812 banns 1754-1822 [Mf 1719]; C 1813-38 MB 1813-37 [Mf 1856]

STALHAM C 1562-1742 M 1562-1740 B 1562-1725 [Mf 1633]

STANFIELD CMB Ext 1560-1752 [20]

STANFORD with STURSTON C 1769-1906 M 1755-1807 1813-1905 B 1769-1911 [Mfc 67261]; CMB 1699-1837 [85]

STANHOE with BARWICK M 1567-1837 [67]; M(I) 1567-1837 [Boyd]

STARSTON M 1561-1642 1661-76 1693-1753 [Mf 1044]; M(I) 1561-1753 [Boyd]

STIBBARD CB 1691-92 1705 1709-10 1715-30 C 1733-1903 M 1705 1715-18 1723-31 M 1733-1978 B 1733-1935 banns 1754-1973 [107]

STIFFKEY with MORSTON CMB 1548-1710 C 1715-1865 M 1715-1919 B 1715-1902 [Mfc 67262]

STODY C 1713-1811 M 1713/14-1811 B 1766-1812 [91]; M(I) 1662-1754 [Boyd]

STOKE FERRY B 1904 [Mfc 92008]; M(I) 1736-54 [Boyd]

STOKE FERRY Oxburgh Hall Cath C 1791-1811 D 1797-1811 [RC/PER]

STOKE HOLY CROSS CB 1538-1812 M 1538-1812 [Mf 1716]; M(I) 1538-1812 [Boyd]

STOKESBY C 1560-1811 MB 1560-1812 banns 1829-42 [Mf 1092]; CMB 1560-1812 [Mf 1090]

STOKESBY with HERRINGBY C 1560-1880 M 1562-1645 1653-1837 banns 1754-1903 B 1560-1643 1652-1927 [Mfc 67263]; M 1560-1812 [60]; M(I) 1561-1812 [Boyd]

STRADSETT CB 1559-1633 M 1559-1622 [Mf 1717]

STRATTON St Mary C 1547-1653 1671-1742 M 1547-1653 1671-1729 B 1547-1653 1671-1726 [Mf 1718]

STRATTON St Michael Cong ZC 1825-37 [80]

STRUMPSHAW M 1562-1812 [AS]; M(I) 1562-1812 [Boyd]

SUFFIELD CMB 1726-1812 [90]; M 1739-1810 [83]

SURLINGHAM M 1561-1646 1656-1811 [Mf 1092]; M(I) 1561-1811 [Boyd]; Z 1561-74 C 1574-1889 M 1561-1889 banns 1860-90 B 1561-1890 B 1704-18 [Mf 1089]

SUSTEAD C 1725-1811 M 1726-1811 B 1726-1812 [86]

SUTTON C 1576-1812 M 1559-1664 1696-1836 B 1564-1812 1845 [Mf 995]; M 1559-1812 B 1755-1802 [Mf 1043]

SWAFFHAM C 1559-1900 M 1559-1900 banns 1805-1905 B 1559-1901 [Mfc 74283 & 79742]; CB 1559-1812 M 1559-1829 [Mf 1701]; CB Ext 1587-1682 [20]; M 1559-1827 [66]; M(I) 1599-1837 [Boyd]

SWAFIELD C 1725-32 1737-1812 M 1725-35 1743-89 1794-1811 B 1725-31 1737-89 1794-1811 [107]; CMB 1660-1812 [Mf 988]; M(I) 1660-1812 [Boyd]

SWAINSTHORPE C 1559-1734 M 1558-1733 B 1558-1731 [Mf 1703]; M(I) 1559-1767 [Boyd

SWANINGTON B 1884 [Mfc 78023]; C 1539-1812 M 1540-1812 B 1538-1812 terrier 1729 [Mf 1088]; C 1540-1751 1812-82 M 1540-1837 B 1538-1812 banns 1754-1816 1824-1910 [Mfc 67264]; C(I) 1539-1812 M(I) 1540-1812 B(I) 1538-1812 [Mf 1088]

SWANTON ABBOT M(I) 1540-1837 [Boyd]; Z 1653-59 C 1538-1812 M

1538-1641 1676-1838 B 1538-1643 1654-1812 [Mf 995]

SWANTON MORLEY CB 1784-1891 M 1755-189 [95]

SWARDESTON CB 1904 [Mfc 92008]; C 1538-1754 M 1538-1711 B 1538-1697 [Mf 1702]

SYDERSTONE CB 1558-1840 M 1587-1674 1683-1840 [23]; CMB 1585-1633 [72]; M 1585-1837 [63]; M(I) 1586-1837 [Boyd]

TASBURGH CMB 1558-1724 [Mf 1704]

TASBURGH SFrs M(I) 1813-37 [PER]

TATTERFORD C 1560-1756 1765-1811 M 1560-1753 1761-1954 B 1560-1756 1765-1812 banns 1762-1831 [Mfc 67265]; C Ext 1561-1765 [Mf 1419]; C 1726-1802 1807-11 M 1725-56 1761-67 1773-81 1787 1798-1802 1811 B 1725-42 1747-1810 [107]; CB 1561-1765 M 1561-1730 [Mf 1090]; M 1561-75 1581-88 1896-1606 1613-41 1649-57 1665-1837 157 [61]; CB 1904 [Mfc 92008]; M(I) 1561-1837 [Boyd]

TATTERSETT CB 1904 [Mfc 92008]; C 1760-1905 M 1755-1812 1835-1902 B 1760-1908 [Mfc 67266]; M 1755-1837 [61]; M(I) 1710-1837 [Boyd]

TAVERHAM CB 1884 [Mfc 78023]; CMB 1601-1837 [49]; M(I) 1720-53 [Boyd]

TERRINGTON St John CB 1884 [Mfc 78023]

THELVETON M(I) 1539-1753 [Boyd]

THETFORD M(I) 1653-1751 [Boyd]

THETFORD St Cuthbert C 1672-1837 M 1673-1837 B 1737-1837 [Mf 1638]

THETFORD St Mary C 1666-1838 M 1666-1837 B 1666-1839 [Mf 1637]; CB 1653-1726 CM 1733-1913 M 1653-1714 1724-27 banns 1754-99 1823-1903 B 1733-1902 [Mfc 67267]

THETFORD St Mary with St Cuthbert & St Peter ZMB 1653-69 [Mf 1635]

THETFORD St Peter C 1672-1838 MB 1672-1837 [Mf 1636]

THETFORD Ind Meeting House CB 1822-38 [Mfc 91250]

THETFORD Wes Meth B 1830-37 [Mfc 91246]

THOMPSON CB 1538-1812 M 1538-

1754 [Mf 1705]

THORNAGE CB 1892 [Mfc 78023]; CMB 1696-1812 [89]

THORNHAM CB 1873 [Mfc 92008]

THORPE ABBOTS M(I) 1564-1758 [Boyd]; CMB 1560-1727 [Mf 1857]

THORPE HAMLET CB 1884 1887 1891-92 [Mfc 78023]

THORPE MARKET C 1538-1739 M 1537-1642 1654-1733 B 1554-1739 1834 1865 [Mf 996]; C 1540-1739 M 1538-44 1557-60 1575 1584 1613-37 1660-96 1706/07-32 B 1556-1737 [Mf 1088]; C(I) 1538-1739 [Mf 1419]; CMB 1726-1812 [87]; M(I) 1539-1739 [Boyd]

THORPE NEXT HADDISCOE St Matthias M Ext 1655-1753 [Mf 1095]

THORPE NEXT NORWICH C 1642-1812 M 1671-1812 B 1673-1812 [Mf 1088]

THREXTON CMB 1602/03-28/29 [49]

THRIGBY C 1539-1730 1747-1812 M 1540-1680 1690-1726 1739-1836 banns 1844 1898-1952 B 1539-1677 1688-1714 1726-27 1749-1804 [Mfc 67268]; CB 1539-1812 M 1539-1812 [Mf 1090]; M 1539-1812 [60]; M(I) 1540-1812 [Boyd]

THURGARTON CMB 1725-1812 [90]; M 1755-1811 [Mf 1706]

THURLTON C 1558-1840 1845 M 1558-1627 1640-1836 B 1558-1840 [45]; M 1538-39 1560-1627 1640-1714 [Mf 1095]

THURNE M(I) 1559-1837 [Boyd]

THURNE with OBY & ASHBY M 1559-1649 1656-65 1672-1837 179 [62]

THURNING CB 1891 [Mfc 78023]

THURSFORD M 1692-1837 [61]; M(I) 1692-1837 [Boyd]

THURTON CB 1904 [Mfc 92008]

THWAITE St Mary M 1539-1837 [60]; M 1545-1834 [55]; M(I) 1545-1837 [Boyd]

TIBENHAM C 1560-1928 M 1560-1903 B 1560-1889 [Mfc 75758]

TITTLESHALL with GODWICK St Mary CB 1539-1904 M 1538-1661 1714-25 1731-1901 banns 1755-1812 1825-82 [Mfc 89549]

24

TIVETSHALL St Margaret C 1673-1837 M 1680-1837 B 1678-1837 [109]; M(I) 1680-1754 [Boyd]

TIVETSHALL St Mary C 1672-1837 M 1674-1837 B 1678-1837 Norfolk registers vol. 13 [112]; M(I) 1674-1754 [Boyd]

TOFT MONKS CB 1904 [Mfc 92008]

TOFTREES CB Ext 1769-1806 [20]; CMB 1739-40 1746-47 [Mf 987]; M 1754-1837 [61]; M(I) 1757-1834 [Boyd]

TOFTS, WEST with BUCKENHAM PARVA alias TOFTS C 1734-1904 M 1735-1903 banns 1762-1900 B 1733-1907 [Mfc 67269]; CMB 1705-1837 [85]

TOMPSON CB 1884 [Mfc 78023]

TOPCROFT M 1557-1813 [60]; M(I) 1557-1812 [Boyd]

TOWN BARNINGHAM see BARNINGHAM WINTER

TRIMINGHAM C 1557-1700 1740-1840 M 1557-1646 1656 1686 1739 1748-68 1774-1836 B 1557-1700 1749-1840 [45]; C 1557-1700 1740-1840 M 1557-1686 1739 1748-1836 B 1557-1700 1749-1840 [Mf 1088]; C 1725-1802 M 1731-1802 B 1726-1802 [87]; CMB 1691-1752 [Mf 996]

TROWSE C 1706-25 B 1696-1724 [Mf 1707]

TROWSE NEWTON M(I) 1695-1749 [Boyd]

TRUNCH C(I) 1558-1812 [Mf 1419]; CMB 1558-1812 M 1813-37 banns 1755-1812 [Mf 996]; CMB 1725-1812 [90]

TUDDENHAM, EAST C 1561-1752 M 1561-1747 B 1561-1751 [32]; M(I) 1561-1747 [Boyd]

TUDDENHAM, NORTH C 1560-1725 1788 M 1560-1753 B 1560-1725 [Mf 1709]

TUNSTALL CB 1557-1812 [Mf 1710]

TUNSTEAD C 1678-1901 M 1678-1902 B 1678-1908 [Mfc 67270]; CMB 1677-1725 [Mf 1634]

UPTON B 1558-1701 [Mf 987]; CMB Ext 1558-1698 [Mf 1046]; M 1558-1812 [AS]; M(I) 1558-1812 [Boyd]

UPWELL CB 1904 [Mfc 92008]

WACTON C 1560-1902 M 1560-1650 1661-1700 1717-1836 banns 1824-82 B 1553-1703 1715-1812 [Mfc 67271]

WALCOT C 1559-1710 1745-1812 M 1558-1711 1745-1836 B 1558-1812 [Mf 996]; C Ext 1559-1812 M Ext 1559-1753 B Ext 1558-1812 [Mf 1096]; M(I) 1558-1837 [Boyd]

WALPOLE St Peter CB 1884 1887 B 1890 [Mfc 78023]

WALSHAM, NORTH C 1557-1812 M 1653-1837 B 1541-1812 [Mf 1003-4]; M(I) 1541-1837 [Boyd]

WALSHAM, SOUTH St Laurence CB 1884 1887 1890-92 1894 B 1893 [Mfc 78023]; C 1551-1756 M 1550-1745 B 1550-1755 [Mf 1046]; M(I) 1550-1756 [Boyd]

WALSHAM, SOUTH St Mary C 1551-1738 M 1550-1669 1684-1743 B 1550-1738 [Mf 1046]; CB 1884 1890-94 [Mfc 78023]; C(I) 1551-1743 [Mf 1419]; M(I) 1550-1750 [Boyd]

WALSINGHAM, GREAT C 1558-1870 M 1559 1566-1901 B 1558-1898 [Mfc 67272]

WALSINGHAM, LITTLE C 1558-1733 1873-77 M 1558-1733 1788-1812 1837-1901 banns 1788-1832 B 1558-1678 1873-75 1885-1901 [Mfc 67273]

WALSOKEN B 1884 1886-87 1890-94 [Mfc 78023]; C 1572-1850 M 1572-1868 banns 1822-75 B 1572-1875 [Mf 2194-95]

WALTON, EAST C 1560-66 1585-91 1607-31 1670-1782 M 1562-66 1585-91 1609-31 1671-1754 B 1563-66 1586-91 1607-31 1670-1782 [Mf 1087]; M 1560-1631 1671-1836 [65]; M(I) 1562-1837 [Boyd]

WATERDEN C 1730-94 1801-37 M 1743-50 1848-50 B 1775-89 1800-13 1819-36 [83]; C 1778-1810 M 1778-1811 B 1781-1809 [97]; M 1743-1812 [63]; M(I) 1743-1812 [Boyd]

WATTON Ind Chapel C 1822-37 [86]

WAXHAM C 1780-1812 B 1786-1812 [Mf 994]; C Ext 1780-1854 M Ext 1758-1834 B Ext 1789-1871 [Mf 1095]; C 1780-1991 M 1755-1988 B 1786-1985 [97]

WEASENHAM All Saints C 1568-1812

M 1569-1812 B 1561 1568-1812 [Mf 987]; C 1568-1812 MB 1569-1812 [Mf 1713]

WEASENHAM St Peter C 1581-1750 1783-1809 M 1581-1812 B 1581-1740 1783-1812 [Mf 1712]

WEETING All Saints M 1561-1653 [59]; M(I) 1561-1812 [Boyd]

WEETING St Mary M 1558-1746 [59]; M(I) 1558-1750 [Boyd]

WELLINGHAM C 1756 1777-1921 M 1765-1902 banns 1824-1911 B 1756 1778-1904 [Mfc 67274]; CMB 1746-47 [Mf 987]

WELLS Ind Meeting House B 1813-37 [Mfc 91250]

WELLS SFrs M(I) 1813-37 [PER]

WELLS NEXT THE SEA B 1659-1900 [108]; C Ext 1659-1753 [113]; M 1659-1754 [112]

WELNEY CM 1834 [Mfc 92008]; M 1653-1753 [CA/R 15]; M(I) 1653-1753 [Boyd]

WELNEY St Mary the Virgin M 1813-95 [86]

WENDLING CB 1890-94 [Mfc 78023]; CMB Ext 1539-1677 [20]

WEREHAM CMB 1834 [Mfc 92008]; M 1558-1683 1697-1753 [Mf 1087]; M(I) 1558-1753 [Boyd]

WESTACRE M 1665-1837 [65]

WESTFIELD CMB 1834 [Mfc 92008]

WESTON LONGVILLE C 1660-1877 M 1660-1835 B 1660-1928 [Mfc 94279]

WESTWICK CMB 1834 [Mfc 92008]; C 1642-1812 M 1642-1836 B 1642-1811 1734 1791 [Mf 991]; CM 1642-1811 banns 1817-38 B 1643/44-1811 [Mf 1087]; M(I) 1642-1836 [Boyd]

WEYBOURNE CMB 1729-1812 [89]

WHEATACRE CMB 1834 [Mfc 92008]

WHEATACRE BURGH *see* BURGH ST PETER

WHINBURGH CMB 1834 [Mfc 92008]

WHISSONSETT M 1700-1837 [63]; M(I) 1700-1837 [Boyd]

WHITWELL C 1559-1783 1813-88 M 1559-1903 B 1559-1783 1814-1908 [Mfc 66600]

WICKLEWOOD CMB 1834 [Mfc 92008]

WICKMERE CB 1665-1812 M 1670-

1810 [92]

WICKMERE with WOLTERTON CB 1893 [Mfc 78023]

WIGENHALE St Mary C 1558-1746 M 1558-1771 B 1558-1749 1782 [Mf 1093]

WIGGENHALL CB 1885-86 1894 [Mfc 78023]

WIGGENHALL St Mary the Virgin CMB 1558-1654 [50]

WILDY & HARGHAM CMB 1834 [Mfc 92008]

WILBY CB 1541-1733 M 1543-1733 [Mf 1711]

WILTON M 1634-1837 [90]; M(I) 1640-1700 [Boyd]

WIMBOTSHAM CMB 1834 [Mfc 92008]

WINCH, EAST CB 1884-87 1890-94 B 1888-89 [Mfc 78023]; M 1690-1837 [65]; M(I) 1690-1838 [Boyd]

WINCH, WEST CB 1884-87 1889-90 [Mfc 78023]; CMB 1559-1812 [Mf 1715]

WINFARTHING CMB 1834 [Mfc 92008]; M(I) 1614-1754 [Boyd]

WINTERTON M 1747-1837 [62]; M(I) 1717-1837 banns 1626-1785 [Boyd]

WINTERTON with EAST SOMERTON C Ext 1717-1812 M Ext 1747-71 B Ext 1747-1812 [Mf 1043]; M 1747-1837 [62]; C 1717-1812 M 1754-1813 B 1747-1812 [Mf 988]

WITCHINGHAM, GREAT CMB 1836 CB 1885 [Mfc 78023]; M(I) 1539-1752 [Boyd]

WITCHINGHAM, LITTLE CMB 1836 [Mfc 78023]; M(I) 1565-1753 [Boyd]

WITTON by BLOFIELD CMB 1836 [Mfc 78023]; M 1582-1812 [AS]

WITTON C Ext 1561-1853 M Ext 1559-1753 1794-1849 B Ext 1558-1855 [Mf 1087]; CMB 1558-1903 [Mf 1005]

WITTON near NORTH WALSHAM CMB 1834 [Mfc 92008]; M(I) 1582-1812 [Boyd]

WITTON near NORWICH M(I) 1558-1837 [Boyd]

WIVETON CMB 1832 1836 B 1883 [Mfc 78023]

WOLFERTON CMB 1832-33 1836 [Mfc 78023]; M(I) 1655-1812 [Boyd]

WOLTERTON see WICKMERE
WOLTERTON C 1720-64 M 1719-63 B 1719-47 [91]
WOLVERTON M 1653-1656 1671-74 1690-1812 [AS]
WOOD DALLING CMB 1653-1812 [Mf 1005]; CMB 1828-30 1832-33 1836 CM 1834 CB 1883 [Mfc 78023]
WOOD NORTON CMB 1828-30 1832-34 1836 CB 1886 1893 [Mfc 78023]
WOOD RISING CMB 1834 [Mfc 92008]
WOODBASTWICK & PANXWORTH M 1561-1813 [AS]
WOODBASTWICK C 1560-1920 M 1561-1840 B 1558-1813 CMB(I) 1560-1812 [Mfc 67275]; CMB 1828 1830 1832-33 [Mfc 78023]; M(I) 1561-1812 [Boyd]
WOODRISING C 1561-1678 1695-1783 M 1562-1678 1695-1748 B 1564-1678 1695-1782; [52]; CB 1783-1812 M 1759-77 1786-1811 1813-36 banns 1786-1819 [110]
WOODTON CMB 1834 [Mfc 92008]; M 1538-1812 [60]; M(I) 1538-1811 [Boyd]
WOOTTON, NORTH CMB 1826 1828-30 1832-34 1836 [Mfc 78023]; M 1655-1837 [64]; M(I) 1655-1837 [Boyd]
WOOTTON, SOUTH CMB 1826 1828-30 1832-36 [Mfc 78023]; M 1556-1837 [64]; M(I) 1557-1837 [Boyd]
WORMEGAY CMB 1834 [Mfc 92008]; C 1565-1614 M 1565-1643 B 1565-1648 [Mf 1093]
WORSTEAD CMB 1834 [Mfc 92008]; C 1558-1901 M 1558-1901 B 1558-1667 1678-1884 [Mfc 67276]; C 1562-1812 M 1562-1884 B 1600-1812 [Mf 1044]; M(I) 1558-1837 [Boyd]
WORTHING CMB 1826 1828-36 B 1827 [Mfc 78023]
WORTWELL with HARLESTON Ind Chapel B 1810-36 [Mfc 91249]
WRAMPLINGHAM CMB 1834 [Mfc 92008]; M 1566-1725 1741-47 [Mf 1087]; M(I) 1567-1747 [Boyd]

WRENINGHAM CMB 1834 [Mfc 92008]
WRETHAM, EAST & WEST CB 1834 [Mfc 92008]; C 1748-1891 M 1754-37 banns 1754-1811 1823-1903 B 1748-1812 [Mfc 67277]
WRETHAM, WEST CMB 1745-47 [Mf 987]
WRETTON M 1697-1770 [Mf 1087]; M(I) 1697-1770 [Boyd]
WROXHAM CMB 1826-36 [Mfc 78023]
WYMONDHAM M(I) 1813-37 [73]
WYMONDHAM Ind Cong C 1754-1822 B 1754-1838 [83]
WYMONDHAM SFrs M(I) 1813-37 [PER]
YARMOUTH, GREAT B 1721-54 [84]; C 1559-1782 M 1558-1661 1677-1782 M(I) 1558-1814 B 1558-1691 [Mf 997-1002]; C 1721-54 M 1721-54 [14]; CM(I) 1721-54 [15-16]; M 1665-1714 1799-35 D 1795-1835 [Mf 989]; M(I) 1558-1758 [Boyd]; Z 1653-65 CMB 1558-1767 CB 1767-1806 C 1806-27 1872-83 1890-1901 M 1767-1837 B 1801-12 1819-1901 CMB 1826-37 CB 1842-59 1883-94 B 1860-73 B 1799-1802 [Mfc 78023]
YARMOUTH, GREAT St Andrew C 1889-1901 [Mfc 78023]
YARMOUTH, GREAT St George C 1894-1901 [Mfc 78023]
YARMOUTH, GREAT St Nicholas C Ext 1570 1583-96 1627-29 1646-59 1670-1781 M Ext 1559-1676 1714-16 [Mf 1081]; C 1804-20 [98-99]; C(I) 1799-1803 [95]; C(I) 1821-24 M(I) 1807-37 B(I) 1800-37 [101-105]
YARMOUTH, GREAT Ind C 1643-1705 D 1650-1704 [PER]
YARMOUTH, GREAT Old Meeting Presb Gaol Street B 1800-37 [Mfc 91240]
YARMOUTH, GREAT St Peter C 1895-1901 [Mfc 78023]
YAXHAM C 1688-1723 1782 M 1695-1734 B 1686-1729 [Mf 1714]
YELVERTON M(I) 1559-97 1698-1767 [Boyd]

NORFOLK - MARRIAGE LICENCES

Calendar to the marriage licences, Archdeaconry of Norfolk, 1576/7-89 and calendar to marriage licences, Norfolk Consistory Court, 1579-88 [ML/GEN]

A collection of pedigrees of Norfolk & Suffolk families, wills & marriage licences: Campling collection [Mf 953-962]

Index to marriage licence bonds 1624-1860 in Norfolk peculiar jurisdictions NF/PER]

Marriage licence bonds of the Suffolk Archdeaconry Registry at Ipswich 1663-1750 [ML/SUF]

Marriage licences from the official note books of the Archdeaconry of Suffolk, deposited at the Ipswich probate court, 1675-1707 [SF/R 273]

Marriage licences of the Archdeaconry of Suffolk deposited at Ipswich Probate Court, 1613-74 [SF/R 272 & ML/SUF]

Marriage licences of the Consistory Court at Norwich, 1563-88, A-Bra only [AS]

Marriage licences of the Consistory Court at Norwich, 1563-88: index [ML/NOR]

Norfolk & Suffolk marriage licences from the Campling Collection; 16th to 18th centuries vol. 1 [ML/GEN]

Norfolk Archdeaconry marriage licence bonds 1813-37 [NF/PER]

HAVE YOU FOUND ALL THE PLACES THAT INTEREST YOU IN THIS BOOKLET?

If the answer to this question is "No", then perhaps you might consider helping the Society of Genealogists to improve its collection of registers. You can do this by sponsoring the purchase of material for the place in which you are interested. It is often possible for the Society to obtain microfiche or microfilm copies of original registers from County Record Offices or other sources. Sponsors share the costs of these acquisitions with the Society.

For further details, please complete the form below and return it to
The Librarian
Society of Genealogists
14 Charterhouse Buildings
Goswell Road
London EC1M 7BA

Name: _____

Address: _____

_____

_____

Daytime Telephone no.: _____ Membership no.: _____

I am interested in the Society's sponsorship scheme and would like further information. I am especially interested in the parishes of:

_____ in _____ (County)

_____ in _____ (County)

_____ in _____ (County)

_____ in _____ (County)

Signed: _____ Date: _____

County sources at the Society of Genealogists -
Norfolk (July 2000)